SPEND LESS AND RETIRE LIKE A KING

Strategies for getting out of debt and becoming financially free in retirement

David Rye

WESTERN PUBLICATIONS
10271 South 175th Avenue
Goodyear, AZ 85358-5502

1

Contents

Introduction

Unfortunately, tens of millions of baby boomers have a serious debt problem. They're headed for financial disaster if they don't figure out a way to get out of debt. If you're one of them, don't let it destroy your life. As you read *Spend Less and Retire Like a King*, you will quickly learn how to assess the magnitude of your debt problems so that you can determine how you got into debt and, more important, how you can get out of debt. When you plunge into topics like how to avoid debt traps and how to create a realistic spending plan that works for you, you will discover the answers you've been looking for. You'll find out how you can dramatically improve the overall quality of your life once you eliminate your debt load.

With fiscal discipline and a clear plan, you can get out of debt and live debt-free forever. Debt can be a crushing burden, but you don't have to let it destroy your life. With fiscal discipline, you can get out of debt and live debt-free forever. In the easy-to-read, accessible style of *Spend Less and Retire Like a King*, you will find answers hard questions about debt including:

- How to determine if you have a debt problem?

- What exactly is a budget and how do you set one up?

- What three things can you do now to improve your credit score?

- Should you consider getting a debt consolidation loan?

This book contains all of the elements you need to consider to get out of debt and improve your financial well-being. Each chapter builds on what you've learned from the previous chapter. Based upon your own situation, select the chapters that cover subjects that are most important to you. That will allow you to maneuver through your personal debt-related issues and make the right decisions to avoid economic catastrophe. The book is filled with real-world examples and supplemented with detailed "here's why it works" illustrations and related websites you can go to for additional information.

As a bonus, you will learn the secrets of becoming financially independent that are covered in the "Putting Everything Together" chapter at the end of the book. You'll find out how you can dramatically improve the overall quality of your life once you eliminate your debt load. The sooner you start mounting an assault on your personal debt, the sooner you will see your debt numbers heading down rather than up. When that happens, you will feel great. With this book at your side, you can conquer debt and secure your financial future.

Chapter 1

Dealing With Debt

If you want to eliminate debt, then you've got to control your spending

On average, people are spending a scary 20 percent of their disposable income on debt, not counting their mortgage debt. The average American owes $9,000 on their credit cards alone and they're lucky if they a just able to stay ahead of the bills. Only 1 percent of Americans are able to put some money away for savings. On top of all that, every American (man, woman, and child) owes $80,000 to Uncle Sam to pay off our insidious national debt. Over the past five years, the average total household debt including mortgages has soared from 60 percent to 75 percent of annual disposable income. These are just a few of the debt numbers that can make anyone become discouraged.

Debt Basics

Excessive spending is the primary cause of personal debt. It has become as addictive as alcohol or drugs in this country. Like alcohol or drugs, debts can interfere with every aspect of your life including damaging relationships with those who mean the most to you. Americans owe more money now than ever before. As you read through this chapter and assess your current debt situation, take an honest look. What do people who get into debt have in common?

People who get into excessive debt are all addicted to overspending. The inappropriate use of loans and credit cards is one of the primary reasons why people encounter major debt problems. When their wallet is nearly empty and their checkbook balance is low, they should know they're nearing their spending limit. But if they can easily turn to their credit cards, they can go into an overspending mode without realizing it until the bills start coming in.

There are two basic types of debt: unsecured debt and secured debt. Unsecured debts are those that are not backed by collateral. Because there are no assets behind unsecured loans, lenders realize a bigger risk from borrowers and therefore charge a higher interest rate for the loan. Credit card debts and personal loans are examples of unsecured loans. Secured debts are backed with collateral, which reduces a lender's risk. They can therefore charge a lower interest rate for the loan. For this reason, secured debts are considered good or preferred debt over unsecured debts. Home mortgages and most car loans are examples of secured loans.

Do You Have a Debt Problem?

People with serious debt problems often panic and move too fast to solve a problem that has been with them for years. They'll quickly pay off the wrong kinds of debt without assessing their entire financial situation. In most cases, short-term fixes won't make their debt problems disappear. To determine if you have a problem, check the following warning signs. If three or more signs apply, you may have a serious debt problem.

1. Always juggling payments or stalling one creditor to pay another and consistently receiving past due notices on your bills.

2. Failing to save a consistent amount of money each month. You're unable to save at least 5 percent of your paycheck each payday.

3. Charging more each month than you make in debt payments and having more than five credit cards.

4. Taking longer and longer to pay off your debts and using credit card cash advances to make payments on other debt accounts.

5. Always running out of money before payday and bouncing checks on a recurring basis.

6. Not knowing how much money you owe and searching through your junk mail to find applications for new credit cards.

7. Charging purchases like groceries that you used to pay for in cash.

8. Paying the bare minimum allowed on your debts (e.g., credit cards) every month.

Good credit management requires planning and constant monitoring. Take a look at your current credit situation. Do you know how much you payout each month on credit cards and loan obligations? Are your total debts in line with your disposable income, which is the dollars you have left after taxes have been deducted from your paycheck? Do you have money in a savings account that you can use to cover financial emergencies such as a job loss or sudden medical bills?

Your Credit Score

Unfortunately, debt has become the high-octane fuel that powers our economy and funds the lifestyle of many individuals. The advent of consumer credit and the resulting debt has created a system for creating and maintaining a credit score on every debtor in the country. The more you know about your own score and how it's maintained, the better off you will be to make sure it is used in your best interest. If your credit picture isn't clear in your mind, it's time to organize your thoughts and take a closer look at where you're going financially. Overspending and living beyond one's means combined with a lack of awareness, self-control, and commitment will create excessive debt at an alarming pace.

Most loans are based on your credit score, which is a three-digit number that lenders use to help determine your creditworthiness. Credit score is a snapshot of your credit history at any moment in time that indicates to lenders the likelihood you will default on your loan payments. The most common score is known as the Fair Isaac Corporation, or FICO, score that ranges from a low score of 560 points to a high of 800 points. The higher your score, the better will be the interest rates and terms you'll get on a loan. Your credit score is used by the lender to determine how much he is willing to lend you and what interest rate he will charge. Let's say you want to borrow $10,000 for five years to dramatically illustrate how much more you will have to pay if your credit score is low:

Interest Paid on a $10,000 Loan Over Five Year		
Credit Score	Interest Rate Charged	Interest Paid
720-800	6%	$620
700-719	7%	$725
675-699	8%	$825
620-674	10%	$1,035
561-619	14%	$1,445
Below 561	18%	$1,860

Obviously, if your credit score is below the minimum score, a lender won't lend you anything. Your credit score can also affect the rates you'll have to pay for homeowners and auto insurance. It can also affect whether or not you'll get hired for a particular job (for example, a money-handling position). The bottom line is that your credit score is a powerful piece of information that can work for or against you, so manage it well.

If your potential creditors believe that you have accumulated an excessive amount of debt, they will either refuse to extend a loan to you or they will charge you high interest rates. This determination is made from your credit score, which is disclosed to them by credit agencies. Your creditworthiness is based on your payment history, income, potential debt, and the number of years you have been employed. The three major credit bureaus to contact for your credit report are:

Equifax Information Service Center, P.O. Box 740241, Atlanta, GA 30374 (800-686-1111 or *www.equifax.com)*

Experian Consumer Assistance (formerly TRW), P.O. Box 2104, Alien, TX 75013 (800-397-3742 or *www.experian. com)*

Trans Union Corp., Consumer Disclosure Center, P.O. Box 390, Springfield, PA 19064 (800-916-8800 or *www.transunion. com)*

Improving Your Credit Score

What is a good credit score? The qualified answer to that question depends in part on where your score has been, where you want it to go, and how you plan on using it. If your score is less than 625, you will have a difficult time getting a legitimate lender to loan you money. The majority of people have scores that exceed 625. A score of 700 or higher (800 is the highest) is a good credit score. It will allow you to qualify for the best interest rate on both secured and unsecured loans. Higher credit scores are needed to qualify for home mortgages. Lenders are reluctant to give a thirty-year fixed rate mortgage to someone with a low score. Your high score shows that you have "staying power" for a long-term loan. Auto loans are a bit more lenient because they are short-term (six years or less) loans. The more credit cards you have listed on your credit report, the lower your score even if the cards are paid off. That's because they suggest that you can quickly max out your credit limit if you use them. You are better off having just one major credit card.

When you review your credit report, look for errors and outdated information that may be causing your score to be lower than it should be. If you find errors, notify the appropriate bureau in writing of any necessary corrections. Make sure you have a checking and a savings account. Lenders view these accounts as a minimum sign of stability and make sure these accounts are recorded on your credit report. Have at least one credit card that you are using that's in good standing (i.e., no late payments, not maxed out, etc.). If you have a

13

credit score above 620, you will begin to get favorable rates on the money you borrow. You need a score above 720 to qualify for the best rates-though in times of severe credit crunch and even that may not be enough.

Credit bureaus get your credit status from creditors, who report your payment history to the bureaus. If creditors make a mistake, it goes on your record. Minor errors are usually not important, but a major mistake like showing a tax lien against you can take months to resolve and your credit can be cut off while the problem is getting resolved. A recent study by the U.S. Department of Commerce showed that 75 percent of the consumer credit files that they randomly audited contained at least one major error. If you review your credit report for errors, make sure you check the following:

- All of your identification information including your social security number, date of birth, current and past addresses, and current and former employers and their addresses.

- All account numbers, correct account status (active or closed) and your payment record history is correct, with an emphasis on checking late payment marks.

In the event that you discover an error, write the credit bureau to request that the error be corrected. Attach whatever documentation you may have to back up your claim. Under federal law, they are required to respond to your request within thirty days.

Getting Out of Debt

Getting out of debt when you're "up to your neck" in bills may make the goal seem impossible to reach. You may have taken out several easy payment loans when your income was in line with your expenses. But now, with the cost of everything on the rise, those once-easy payments are harder to make. To get out of debt, stop charging your purchases and do not open new credit accounts. If you are not sure you have the willpower to stop charging, remove all of the credit cards in your wallet and cut each one of them into small pieces. Create a spending plan.

A spending plan shows you how you will spend your money on a daily, weekly, and monthly basis. It is itemized down to what you plan to spend on any given day. Do you need one? The answer to the question is an emphatic YES. If you don't have a plan that's dealing with your debt, you will substantially reduce your chances of ever getting out of debt. One of the first things you need to do to set up a spending plan is to determine what your credit limit should be. The total limit available to you may be more than you can handle. It's up to you to establish the credit limit that is acceptable to you and record that number in your plan. To determine your personal credit limit, figure out how much you can afford to pay each month for credit purchases. Review your monthly debt payments as well as your total outstanding debt. Once you establish your personal credit limit, plan your credit spending so that your total payments do not exceed this amount. If you are interested in learning more about "getting out of debt" plans, visit Quicken's website at *www.quicken.com/planning/debt.*

A spending plan is an active strategy you use on a daily basis to help control your spending habits so that you can meet your financial goals. It starts with a commitment you make to yourself, like "I want to save and invest some of my income to live better and become financially independent." When you activate your plan, it will help you discriminate between what you need and what you want. Here are three things a spending plan will help you accomplish:

- It helps you plan and prepare for the big expenses like a new car and helps you eliminate the unnecessary things you might otherwise buy without planning.

- It will help you put more money into your savings account for investments every month. It sets the groundwork for developing a financial plan, your road map to financial independence.

- It gets you used to living on what you make and gets you, your spouse, and your kids pulling in the same financial direction.

15

Is Bankruptcy an Alternative?

If your financial situation seems hopeless, you may want to consider bankruptcy as a way out. Before you file for bankruptcy, discuss the consequences with your spouse, close family members, and friends. Regardless of what you may have heard, bankruptcy is not a simple solution. Your credit rating will be severely tarnished for seven to ten years and you will be required to pay high interest rates on any loans that you're able to get after declaring bankruptcy.

When filing for bankruptcy, you file for a bankruptcy petition under the federal bankruptcy law. Although you can file petition by yourself, you are much better off retaining the services of a bankruptcy attorney. You and your attorney draw up a petition listing your assets and liabilities. You submit the petition to a U.S. District Court judge, and if the judge accepts your petition, some of your assets could be sold by the court to pay off your creditors. The court then wipes out most or all of your debts except:

- Alimony and child support
- Most state and federal taxes
- Most federal student loans
- Any debt not listed on your bankruptcy petition

If you are interested in learning more about bankruptcy, visit the website _www.bankruptcyinfo.com_. Bankruptcy should only be used as a last-ditch effort because it will ruin your credit (FICO) score for years. A bankruptcy stays on your credit report for seven to ten years-that's a long time to go with severely limited credit. Any loans that you might be able to get during this time will likely be charged the highest interest rate that is allowed in your state.

Debts' Impact on Retirement

There's no question that the biggest fear people have when it comes to retirement is financial. Will they have enough money to support themselves and their dependents throughout their retirement years? According to *Forbes* magazine, most people fail to meet their monthly expenses within the first year after they retire. Many retirees fail because they didn't have a plan or specific goals before they retired. Be careful not to fall into that same trap. You can head off the biggest fear by saving enough money to retire comfortably.

Why should you even be thinking about retirement when you're surrounded by debt? Unfortunately, 60 percent of Americans are heavily in debt when they retire. As a result, they are forced to substantially cut back on their standard of living when they retire and many have to work part-time just to make ends meet. The rest generally make a successful transition into retirement because they were debt free. Those who managed their debt and invested their money wisely were able to leave the corporate world and begin enjoying the fruits of their labor.

Whenever you plan to retire, you are bound to encounter some sleepless nights wondering whether or not you'll have enough money to live on for the rest of your life. Will you be able to get your debts under control and invest your money wisely so that you can retire? There are several questions that you need to think about before you retire that will be covered in this chapter. Are you ready to retire and can you afford it? To help you answer the question, following is a questionnaire that looks at some of the questions you may face. Answer yes or no to each question. "Maybe" answers are not allowed.

1.   Have you developed a retirement plan that clearly identifies what you want to accomplish before and after you retire?

2.   Do you know how much money you'll need to support a retirement lifestyle that's acceptable to you?

3.   Have you identified the exact sources of income that you expect to receive after you retire?

4.   Do you have any dependents that you must take care of after you retire?

5. If yes, do you have a plan in place for how you'll handle this?

6. If you retire before you are eligible for Medicare (age sixty-five), will you have medical insurance that covers you?

If this questionnaire created more questions in your mind than answers, you may want to concentrate your efforts on the sections in the book that address your specific concerns. For example, what will you do to cover yourself with health insurance until you reach the Medicare age of sixty-five? Interim health insurance can be a very expensive proposition and you can unfortunately rest assured that the cost of whatever plan you have today will continue to go up every time you renew the policy.

Count the dollars. Make sure you have a solid pension strategy in place and know exactly what you'll need in your retirement plan in order to retire.

Your home. If you own your home and plan to move into a less expensive home as one of your retirement strategies, make sure you earmark the money that you'll save for investments.

Living expenses. Consider how you can lower your living expenses. Do you really need two cars? Do you have to go out to eat as often as you did when you were working? How much can you save by shopping bargains, now that you have the time?

Regardless of where you are in the retirement planning stage (i.e., near-term or long-term), it behooves you to estimate how much income you'll need when you retire. There are dozens of books at your local library that cover every facet of retirement. Almost without exception, they include one or more forms that you fill out to determine your retirement income needs. By balancing your retirement income needs against the financial resources you'll have in place when you retire, such as social security and your company's pension, you can calculate how much capital you'll need to accumulate to supplement any financial shortfalls you might get.

As a rule of thumb, you will probably need income amounting to 70 percent or 80 percent of your current income to retire on. If your home is paid for when you retire, the income percentage drops by at least 20 percent. If you're interested in completing a more complex estimate of what you'll need when you retire, check out *U.S. News & World Report's* retirement calculator on their website at *www.usnews.com*.

Chapter 2

Setting Debt Elimination Goals

A goal is a personal promise you make to yourself that you will do something

People often take a hasty approach in solving their debt problem. As a result, they end up paying off the wrong debts, in the wrong order, and at the expense of more important financial matters. A better approach is to first assess your overall financial situation before you start challenging your debt. You can't make smart debt management decisions in a vacuum. Your other financial goals like retirement can have a profound impact on which debts you pay off and how quickly. Make sure you have enough saved up to cover financial emergencies like car repairs. This chapter will help you determine meaningful debt elimination goals to set.

The two prevalent reasons most people fail to get out of debt are (1) they lack the personal commitment to make it happen and (2) they can't control their excessive spending habit to fit within a standard of living that they can afford. They continue to write checks and charge credit cards without any regard for how they're going to pay for it. They are infatuated with doing whatever it takes to maintain their perceived high standard of living in the short run with little or no thought for the long-term consequences of their actions. They'd rather not think about the long term. Once they get used to their short-term standard of living, they are caught up in a vicious circle.

Understanding Your Debt

How do I start to understand my debts? To get started, you need to know exactly what you owe by account. For each debt, write down the current balance owed and whether the loan is an installment or revolving loan. Revolving debt includes credit cards where you have a credit limit that you can draw on. Paying off revolving loans generally increases your financial flexibility because you can always draw on that freed-up credit line if you need it. What is the interest rate you're paying and is the rate fixed or variable? Credit cards are typically variable since the rates can change at any time. Installment loans usually have a fixed rate unless you took out an adjustable-rate loan (e.g., a home mortgage).

Installment loans include mortgages and car loans where you have a set schedule of payments to make and a specific pay off date. An installment loan is for a specific purpose and is gradually repaid in full-there is no freed-up credit line to draw from. Is the interest on a given loan tax-deductible? If you pay a loan off, are there any prepayment penalties? What is the minimum amount you are allowed to pay for each loan?

Go through your bank statement and write down what you spent your money on over the past three months (e.g., food, entertainment, credit card interest, living expenses, etc.). How much money did you make, and did you have enough to cover all of your expenses? Did you spend more than you made? If you spent less than you made, what did you do with the extra money? That exercise should help you determine where you are today. Now, where do you want to go? Set meaningful, specific financial goals, with a designated completion date assigned to them.

If your goal is to reduce your debt by $10 a day so that you can pay off a credit card, what steps will you take to make it happen and when will you start? If you are living above your means, figure out a way to live within your means. You must figure out how to live on what you make if you want to gain control of your finances.

How Much Money Do You Need?

The answer will be based on how much you need to pay off all your debts, either in a lump sum or in a single monthly payment that you can afford. Let's suppose that you need $10,000 in a lump sum to pay off all your debts (excluding home mortgage) or an additional $200 a month to pay off the same debts in five years. As you proceed through this chapter, you may discover ways to immediately free up some cash to pay off certain debts and ways to refinance part of your debt load. Suppose you were only able to find enough money to cover just a portion of your debts. It's a start, so be positive and move on to the next step.

Find a quiet location where you can be by yourself, sit back, close your eyes, and think. What would your life be like if you were debt free? How would it change your life? Would you be happier? What about your relationships with the people you really care about? If the out-of-debt vision that you create is something that you both want and need, make it the foundation of your drive to get out of debt. Make sure everything you do supports your vision.

Finding the Money

For most people, cutting expenses is a lot easier than raising their income to get out of debt. Name any expense that you have and there is probably a way to reduce it. The following lists will help you get started on expense areas to consider:

Transportation. Increase the deductibles on your auto insurance policy. Start carpooling to work and use public transportation.

Food. Pack a lunch to work and eliminate eating out at fast-food restaurants. Use weekly grocery store circulars to see what's on sale and plan your meals accordingly.

Clothing. Check out consignment and thrift stores for gently used items. Know what looks good on you, and stick to classic styles rather than chasing trends.

At a minimum, you should be able to identify money-saving plays that you can put into your game plan. First determine how you can make some extra money. Getting rid of an unneeded vehicle could allow you to raise some significant cash to retire some of your debts and reduce monthly expenses. Perhaps a yard sale is what you need to get rid of the clutter around the house and make some money at the same time. Have you thought about taking a part-time job? Check out every overtime option where you work. Read the "part time" work ads in the classified sections of the local newspapers to find an opportunity to make some extra money.

Creating a Savings Goal

Most of us have been raised in a "spend it while you got it" society. We were taught that debt was good while savings were not good. The huge buildup of consumer debt has always been a critical component of our national economy. Our entire political system has been geared to endorse our infatuation with debt. Over the past several years, the nation's debt level has climbed from zero dollars to several trillion dollars. The burden of paying that back will fall squarely on your children and grandchildren.

The die-hard savers will argue that the more money you have on hand, the better you can survive a financial emergency without running up more debt. The debt killers will argue that the amount of interest you'll earn in a savings account is usually insignificant in comparison to the interest you're paying on loans. Who's right? Both are. You should begin to develop the discipline it takes to save money (even a small amount) while you're paying off your debts.

Where are you going to find any money to save? If you are like most people, you spend money on things that you really don't need and the money you make is just enough to cover your expenses. Your first challenge will be to get control over your spending habits and establish a monthly budget for everything you buy. You'll be amazed at how it will help you save on the little things that will add up to big dollars over a relatively short period of time. That is where you'll find the money to save.

1. When you get a raise, deposit the extra amount of money you get directly into your savings account so you won't miss it.

2. Take lunches to work instead of eating out and you will be amazed at how much you'll save.

3. When you get your income tax refund, use it to pay off credit cards and then deposit into your savings account the extra money you'll have because you are not making monthly credit card payments.

4. Deposit any part-time money, overtime pay, and bonus checks into your savings account.

5. Pay cash for everything. It is harder to pay cash than it is to use a credit card, and you'll find yourself passing up impulse purchases.

6. Budget a monthly amount to go into a separate savings account for future purchases, such as a car. This can save you thousands later on for interest on a car loan.

Set savings goals, such as "I want to save 1 percent of my income every month." After you prove to yourself that you did that, slap yourself on the back and double your goal to 2 percent. Passbook savings accounts are available in all banks including savings and loan associations and offer the lowest interest rates of all of the savings account vehicles. Use them as a savings vehicle of last resort. They're okay to meet short-term savings needs.

Is the interest rate important, and where should you consider alternative places to put your savings? To answer this question, let's assume you are only able to save $10 a month, or $120 a year, in a 1 percent interest savings passbook account. At the end of the first year, you would have accumulated a whopping $1.20 in interest. The quick and easy answer is that the interest rate is not important, which is the wrong answer. The fact that you managed to save something and earned interest on the money you saved is a significant accomplishment. Had you chosen in this example to save your money in a money market fund, you would have earned five times the interest rate (5 percent) that was earned in a passbook savings account (1 percent). That's important!

Store Your Findings in CDs and MMFs

A certificate of deposit (CD) is money that you deposit with your bank or credit union to hold on your behalf for a specific period of time at a stipulated interest rate. CDs typically pay a much higher interest rate than passbook accounts. The specified time periods that you are required to hold a CD are typically in 90-day increments. For example, you can invest in a 90-day, 180-day, 360-day, or longer CD. The rate of interest that you earn usually increases with the length of time you elect to hold your CD. At the end of whatever time period you choose, your financial institution "cashes out" your CD and issues you a check that covers your principle and earned interest. If for whatever reason you choose to withdraw your funds from a CD before its maturity date, you will pay a penalty. CDs are a very safe place to save money that you're holding for the future. Most banks offer them as a convenience at various amounts and maturity dates.

Money market funds (MMFs) are not mutual funds, as the name would imply. They are checking accounts that are loosely tied to the prevailing interest rate and pay interest that is significantly higher than what you get from a passbook savings account. They are offered through the major banks and mutual fund companies and are government insured. They are a great place to deposit your savings, since they offer the convenience of being able to write a check against your account if you need to access the funds. You are required to maintain a minimum balance in most money market accounts, so check with the financial organizations that interest you.

MMF accounts are a special breed of savings account set up by financial institutions. They pay interest rates that are tied to the overall market interest rates. When you deposit money into an MMF account, your money begins to immediately earn interest at the current money market rate. And you can withdraw part or all of your deposit in an account at any time without incurring an early withdrawal fee. The "no penalty" withdrawal feature gives the edge to MMFs over CDs. Both pay substantially higher interest rates than passbook savings accounts. There is no reason why you would want to keep part or all of your savings in a passbook account over CDs or MMFs.

Avoiding Bad Loans

Throughout, this book implies that all debt is bad and that the less you have, the better off you'll be. However, some debt can do good things to your financial future. For example, a mortgage used to acquire a home provides you with a place to live in an asset that historically increases in value. The interest on home mortgages is tax deductible. An educational loan can boost your (or your kids') income over time. Good debt offers you a favorable return on whatever it is you are financing. Conversely, bad debt does not offer you a favorable return. If you use it to support excessive spending on something that depreciates in value, think twice before you do it.

High-rate loans were once the province of loan sharks and pawnbrokers. Not anymore. Today, high-rate loans are big business. Most of the big banks now make payday loans, tax preparers push refund anticipation loans, and rent-to-own retail outlets offering excessive interest rate loans are in every major city in the country. They all capitalize on people's desire for quick cash, regardless of the cost. Although many of these loans target low-income working people who may feel they have limited options, the promotion schemes are getting more sophisticated and attracting higher income people.

A bad loan has interest rates that exceed the prevailing rates by 20 percent or more and loan terms that include unreasonable late payment penalties, prepayment penalties, or loan costs. Bad becomes worse if you have saddled yourself with payments that you're struggling to meet each month. Ninety percent of the ownership of taking on a bad loan rests with the borrower, not the lender. Lenders may entice you with their ads and twisted words to con you into accepting a loan that's bad for you, but in the end you make the decision. There are the three basic types of loans.

Revolving credit loans allow you to borrow up to a predetermined limit for a defined period of time (e.g., one to five years).The advantage is that these loans are convenient in that you can use them whenever you need money. They charge a stiff interest rate for this convenience.

Installment loans are fixed loan amounts over a specified period of time at a fixed interest rate. They are used to finance large purchases like cars, which are used as collateral for the loan. Therefore, they typically carry a lower interest rate than other loans.

Line of credit loans are secured by an asset (e.g., your home) and therefore charge lower interest rates than the other loan options. Your credit limit is set and you are issued a checkbook when the loan is approved. You can write a check against your credit limit whenever you want.

How do you determine if you have any bad loans? List on a sheet of paper each of your loans, how much you owe, the minimum monthly payment you're allowed to make, and the gross interest rate you are paying. Note the amount of any penalty fees you are charged for late payments. Based upon what you are now paying on a monthly basis, determine when the loan will be paid off. If you need help making that determination, go to the website *www.calculators.usatoday.com* for assistance. With the exception of mortgage debts, any debt that will take you in excess of five years to pay off qualifies as a potential bad loan.

Checking Loan Terms

Don't limit yourself to asking just the questions listed here before you sign loan papers. Ask as many questions as you deem necessary to determine if you should accept the loan. The purpose of these sample questions is to point you in the right direction.

1. What was my credit score and which agency did you get it from?

2. Are there any prepayment penalties, and if so, what are they?

3. What happens if I am late in making a payment?

4. What interest rate will I be charged and how did you arrive at that rate?

5. Are there any conditions within the loan contract that I should particularly be aware of?

Avoid loans with prepayment penalties. Prepayment penalties are stipulated in the loan papers that you sign and specify the fee (penalty) you will be required to pay if you decide to pay off your loan before it is due. Always ask if there is a prepayment penalty before you sign. If there is, read and understand the terms of the penalty. Why would a lender want to charge you additional money to pay off their loan? Because, they want to avoid losing your lucrative business. By charging a prepayment penalty, the lender insures that they make a minimum profit on the loan, even if they don't receive all the interest over the original term. If you elect to pay them their prepayment penalty, the lender still wins. You may say "so what?" because you have no intention of prepaying any loan. But over time, that may change if it is to your financial advantage to pay off a loan.

Is a loan against my retirement account a good idea? It depends. You may be allowed to borrow part of the balance in your retirement account as a loan to yourself with strict stipulations. In most cases, you must repay yourself (i.e., your retirement account) within sixty days from when you withdrew the funds to avoid serious tax penalties. Before you exercise this option, discuss the rules with a person in the organization that administers your retirement plan. Retirement account loans are meant to satisfy short-term needs for cash. Since there is no cost for the loan, they

Inflation's Affect on Debt?

Americans unfortunately have been sucked into the inflation scenario: "Finance now and pay off later with cheaper dollars." That might work if your income increased at the same rate as or a greater rate than inflation. Unfortunately, for most of us, it never has and probably never will. Stagnant economic conditions resulting from significant price spikes in the necessities of life like gasoline and food always add to the debt burden of everybody because inflation erodes the buying power of everybody's paycheck. Don't let yourself get sucked into the "buy it now before the price goes up" hype or you'll just dig yourself into a deeper debt hole.

As you progress through life-which is a diplomatic way of saying "as you get older"-your financial needs will change. When you're young, the last thing you probably want to think about is retiring. You're more concerned about buying a house, raising a family, and acquiring all the material things that you deserve. As you get older, you will face a crossroad in your life. You can either continue to acquire more material things or you can start making an effort to plan for your future by saving money for your retirement. If you wait until you get older to start saving, time is not on your side.

Getting Help

A financial planner makes a living assisting people in developing and implementing customized financial plans. A good financial planner works with you on an ongoing basis to help build your portfolio. Certified financial planners must take a five-part course, pass a ten-hour exam, and complete fifteen hours of additional training a year to become certified. Many financial planners have security licenses, which allow them to sell you the financial products they recommend. Most of us don't need the services of a professional financial planner on an ongoing basis. A periodic consultation with your accountant may be sufficient to manage your debt since basic financial planning isn't hard to do. Under certain circumstances, you may need to work with a financial planner on a recurring basis if:

1. You earn a good wage but cannot manage to save anything on a regular basis, or, to make matters worse, you don't even know where all your money is going.

2. You're facing a tough financial question that you feel can't be answered without some expert advice. For example, your company is "downsizing" and has offered you an early retirement buyout. However, you still have fifteen years left in your career. Should you take it? You may need advice from a financial planner.

3. You've got a savings and retirement plan in place that is just sitting there without any help from you and it's making some money. Should you leave it alone or start playing an active role in managing your investments with the help of a financial planner?

Many banks have money management counselors that are worth talking to. Most big banks are focused on delivering profits to their investors at the expense of the customer service that they're willing to provide for their "regular" customers. Unless you can bring an exceptional amount of business into the bank or make a substantial deposit, you won't have access to their money management staff. Small local and regional banks might offer you more personal finance services and advice. At a minimum, you will need a checking account with some form of overdraft protection, a savings account, direct deposit options, a debit card option as opposed to a credit card, and free access to conveniently located ATMs.

Beware of those "experts" who con people into quick get-out-of debt schemes. Get-rich-quick e-mails, investments that can't lose, gambling, and even chain letters may tempt you off the slow and steady path to getting out of debt. Just remember that every dollar you waste on a fly-by-night solution is a dollar that won't get you closer to your goal. Call the nonprofit Consumer Credit Counseling Service (800-388-CCCS) for help. Most of their 1,300 national offices offer free counseling and will help you trim your expenses, plan a budget, and even help you negotiate better terms from your creditors.

Chapter 3

Spend Less Strategies

If you spend less today, you'll have a lot more to spend tomorrow

Everyone should have a budget to help control what they're spending, even millionaires. It is critical to know where your money is coming from and where it is going. By monitoring your spending habits, you will begin to identify areas where cost savings can occur. You will then be able to create a budget that is conducive to helping you get out of debt and keep your spending on the right track. Many consider budgeting to be a tedious task, but it really doesn't have to be. Once you set one up, it can be easy and even fun to maintain.

Budgeting Basics

Budgeting is an active strategy that you use to get out of debt. It needs to be written down and have simple milestones to show you how you're doing. Budgets are designed to help you gain control over your daily expenses. Excess spending is usually a result of (1) uncontrolled or impulse spending and (2) a failure to realize what you can and cannot afford. Impulse spenders buy first and consider the consequences later. If you are not able to control your daily expenses, then preparing a budget will be a waste of your time. Here are the basic components of a budget:

Disposable income is your gross income less withholdings for taxes, health insurance, FICA, etc.

Major obligations are regular expenses that are usually contractual like rent and mortgage payments, car loans, property taxes, and day care and school expenses. Obligation expenses are anything that must be paid before you can consider other expenses.

Necessities are important expenses such as groceries, utilities, and home maintenance that can be adjusted through tight money management techniques.

Credit card payments are the total monthly payments you need to make on all of your cards.

Discretionary expenses can be significantly modified or eliminated altogether and include entertainment, take-out food, pocket money, family allowances, etc.

Savings is the final component of the budget and shows what you will do with any money that's left over after all expenses have been paid.

The budget is an expanded spending plan in which you methodically project what your anticipated income and expenses will be over a specified period of time. This is typically done on a monthly basis. Record everything you buy in a budget book so you know where you are at any time during the month. This will help keep you from getting that surprised look on your face at the end of the month when you get your bills and say, "Wow, I didn't realize I spent that much." Put a limit on what you are willing to charge each month and stick to it. Pay off the balance that you run up at the end of every month.

Setting One Up

Most budgets fail because they never really get started. Here is what happens in a typical "yeah, let's go on a budget" scenario. In their excitement to figure out a way to get out of debt, people often buy a "how to set up a budget" book and hastily create a budget. A short time later, they may actually sit down and review what they actually spent versus what they said they would spend in their budget. When budget dollars don't match actual dollars, they quickly conclude that the budget idea was just a waste of time, and they go back to doing what they have always done running up more debt. Here are the five steps that you need to take to setup a budget:

Step 1: Understand where your income comes from and where it goes. What about the income that you may receive periodically from sources such as tax refunds, overtime, or a garage sale? How do you plan to use it in your budget? The same goes for unplanned expenses like repairs on your car. Are those types of expenses addressed in your budget?

Step 2: What are your short-term and long-term budget goals? For example, if you are planning to buy a new television with cash, do you have an entry in your budget that shows how much you plan to save each payday to make that happen?

Step 3: Do you have a savings mechanism set up in your budget? For example, if you plan to create an emergency savings account to cover such things as unexpected car repairs, have you opened a savings account for that purpose?

Step 4: Most of us need some amount of pocket money to fund everyday expenses. Address how much each member of your family needs and gets in separate lines within your budget.

Step 5: Review your budget on a regular basis (at least once a week is recommended). Compare actual sources of incoming income against expenses. Were your income and expenses in line with what you forecast in your budget? If you were over or under budget, what happened and what is your plan of action?

After you complete your budget, you should see some money saving areas that you can tackle right away. Identify what are necessary expenses and what are luxury expenses. For example, does each family member really need a cell phone? Do you truly need the most expensive cable television package? Review your miscellaneous spending. Is there anything you can do away with? Do you see any patterns in your spending behavior that you can address? Prioritize your budget. List your expenditures from the most important to the least important. Then assess what you can do away with or cut back on.

One of the best ways to maintain a budget is to find a good budgeting tool that you can use right away. For example, SimplePlanning.com at *www.simpleplanning.net* has a program that is downloadable for a small fee. If you are using Microsoft Office, consider using the financial templates that are included in the program. Any financial planning tool that will help organize your spending and make the process less demanding on your personal time is worthwhile.

Your budget needs to be in writing. You may think you can remember it all, but having it written down is a much more effective method. Every time you review it by yourself or with family members, you will want to record actual income and expense figures next to your budgetary figures. In some cases, you may be able to take immediate action to mitigate a budget problem. Your action plan needs to be spelled out in your budget as a reminder not to repeat the same mistakes in the future.

No budget is going to work if you don't have a commitment from everybody in your family to support it. As a general rule, people are much more willing to endorse a solution to a problem if they are involved in coming up with the solution. Actively solicit their thoughts and incorporate any of their helpful ideas in your final budget. Make sure that everyone who's involved in the process understands that no budget is final. It has to be a dynamic tool that can and will change over time. Let your family know that you want them to be actively involved in those changes. Rewards for their help and commitment like going out to the family's favorite restaurant can help.

Symptoms of Overspending

When your wallet is nearly empty and your checkbook balance is low, you know you're nearing your spending limit. But if you can easily turn to credit, you are more likely to overspend without realizing it until the bills start coming in. Most financial counselors recommend that you should stop charging when your credit payments (not including a mortgage) approach 15 percent of your take-home pay. If you're beyond that, you have fallen into the debt trap.

If your friends tell you that if you borrow what you need, you don't need a budget. What exactly does that mean? That means your friend probably has a lot of debt. Do you know someone who likes to brag about borrowing whatever he or she needs? She will tell you that is why she doesn't need a budget and that is why she's buried in debt. The question that she should be asking is how much she can afford to borrow. If she wanted to get out of debt, then her answer should probably be zero. Be extremely wary of increasing any expense that pushes you further into debt.

People who are always in debt refuse to set up and actively maintain a monthly budget. The term "budgeting" makes their blood run cold. You'll often hear them say, "There is no way I will ever start maintaining a budget because I don't want to know how bad off I am financially." Unless you were raised by financially conscious parents, the disciplinary act of budgeting and being accountable for what you spend is a scary process for most people to consider. For many, it uncovers the reality that they don't have enough money to make ends meet. Overspending demands that they need to immediately start spending less, that they stop buying all the things that they believe they can't live without. Unfortunately, they are not willing to do that and would prefer to remain in debt for the rest of their lives. You can view a sample budget on the Internet at *www.personalbudgeting.com*.

People typically overspend because they buy a lot of stuff that they really don't need. Competing with the Joneses is one reason. There is always a "latest and greatest" product that some people must have regardless of the cost. For example, look at how flat-screen televisions have expanded in size and cost the past couple of years. Or the latest, hottest, fastest computer and cell phone technology. One of the keys in controlling debt is to hold off on any frivolous spending. Apply any extra money you may have to paying off your debt before you accumulate more debt. According to *SmartMoney* magazine, in 2009 the debt per American household (excluding mortgages) is $21,900. Avoid this trap by adhering to your budget.

Cut Back Strategies

To figure out a way to start spending less, you must first know what you're spending now. Although this may sound like a no-brainer, many people don't fully comprehend that they spend more money than they make. A survey conducted by *Money* magazine revealed over half of the people surveyed don't pay off their credit card bills each month, 70 percent don't save on a regular basis, and 60 percent don't want to know how bad off they are financially. Inappropriate use of credit and loans can become one of your biggest financial downfalls. To determine whether you spending too much, check the following warning signs to see if any apply to you:

- You're always juggling payments or stalling one creditor to pay another.

- You're consistently receiving past due notices on your bills.

- You're failing to save a set amount of money each month.

- You're charging more each month than you make in monthly payments.

- You're taking longer and longer to pay off your debts.

If you have a spending problem, what can you do to get your expenses in line with what you make? This is where your budget will come in handy. Understanding your expenses and where they are coming from is your first step in getting them under control. The budget will help you to outline your expenses and identify any areas that can be eliminated. For example, do you really need to have Starbucks coffee every day? At $3 a day, that's $1,095 a year! Budgeting will also flag some necessary expenses, and you can begin to think about how you can decrease or eliminate them.

There are immediate steps can you take now to stop borrowing. Start by assessing every loan to be sure it addresses a valid need in your life. Why do we borrow money? Most of the time, it is because we want something. On occasion, we borrow money because we need something. There is a huge difference between the words "want something" and "need something." You *need* to understand that difference if you want to gain control over your borrowing habits. For example, you may need a car or some other form of transportation to get to work. That's a necessity. However, what you want overrides your need. You *want* a new car, complete with a powerful engine that is capable of catapulting you from zero to 60 miles per hour in less than five seconds. People borrow money to buy what they want, rather than what they need, without regard to the consequences. Stop borrowing for stuff you just want. If you really want it badly enough, save the cash to buy it! A typical new car loan now takes five to six years to pay back. Do you have a savings account set up to cover you for emergencies during those years?

Being a renter can be very frustrating. Every time you turn around, you are plagued with an increase in rent. There are several things you can do that will help you keep your rent cost down. Rent from a private party whenever possible. If you rent from a corporation that owns the property and hires a property manager where everything is run by a computer, you are more likely to face automatic, periodic rent increases. If you rent from an individual who values you as a good renter, they may be less inclined to automatically increase your rent.

Get to know your landlord as a friend, rather than a bill collector. Land lording is a tough job, and if you can establish a solid relationship, he will be more likely not to increase your rent. Don't ask your landlord to do anything that you can do yourself, as long as it is within reason. If the sink or toilet is plugged, unplug it yourself. If a wall needs painting and the landlord has no problem with you painting it, do it yourself and then in a subtle way, let your landlord know how self-sufficient you are. He'll appreciate it. Always pay your rent on time. Landlords have bills to pay that are dependent upon getting their rent checks on time. Keep your place neat. Landlords like to rent to people who will take care of their property.

What can you do to control your urge to always want to spend money? For many, shopping has become a social event, a chance to get out and explore the wonderful world of capitalism and consumerism. Here are several spending excuses to avoid that will help you keep more of your hard-earned money in your wallet, rather than in the retailer's cash register.

- "I'll have the money by the time I have to pay off the loan, and that is why I want to buy it now." Don't buy it until you have the money in hand. That will allow you time to think about the purchase to determine if it is something you really need.

- "I have to have it because this completes the set." We seem duty bound to match things we already have, even if we don't need or want them. Don't buy it just because it completes a set unless it is something that you use on a routine basis.

- "I'm worth it, and therefore I deserve it." If you're about to buy something you have always wanted but don't need, forget it! The fact that you are worth it and deserve it doesn't answer the basic question. Do you really need it?

- "The price is going up." Salespeople know that this old trick is one of the best ways to hook a tentative customer. Don't bite on the "going up" bait! Chances are it will be there tomorrow at the same or a lower price.

At the end on the month when you review what you actually spent versus what you had budgeted to spend, on the minor stuff, take notes and move on to the bigger issues. For example, many utility bills are impossible to estimate to the penny. The fact that your electric bill was $20 over what you had budgeted is not a major budget issue. Simply make a note of it and determine whether you want to increase the budget amount next month or implement a plan to use less electricity. On the other hand, if the minimum payment on one of your credit cards increases by $20 from $100 to $120, take notice. That same $20 increase probably occurred because major debt of several hundred dollars was added to the total balance due on the card. Where did it come from, and was it a result of unplanned expenses? How did it happen? These are just a few of the tough budget questions you need to address before you can implement a preventive plan.

Solicit family participation. Anyone who is spending part of your family's money has to be involved in your spend-less plan or it will probably fail. They can't support a plan they don't know about, so start by showing it to them. To grab their attention, state why you've created this plan. Don't sugarcoat your reasons. Tell them the truth: "It is absolutely essential that we reduce what we are all spending on a daily basis or we will destroy this family's financial future." After you have made your opening statement, wait patiently for a response before you proceed. If anyone doesn't understand the importance of what you're trying to tell them, start over again with a new or revised opening statement. Once you've got their attention, solicit their ideas and their participation in implementing the plan.

Credit Cards

When consumer credit cards first came out in the early seventies, they were considered a status symbol. Your status increased in direct proportion to the number of cards you had. Today, over 50 million credit card charges are made every day, averaging $80 a transaction. Credit cards are the high-octane fuel that is powering the debt overload in today's economy. Paying with cash like our parents used to do is not in our DNA anymore. We replaced cash with a plastic card.

What's the difference between a debit card and a credit card? They look the same but they have different effects on your overall debt. When you apply a purchase against a debit card, you are immediately paying electronically from funds that are linked to the card, like your checking account. You are in effect paying cash for the purchased items and are incurring no additional debt. It's easier than writing out a check. With a credit card, the sponsor of the card (usually a bank) pays for the purchases you made against the card. You pay the card company back with interest at a later date. Debit card spending is limited to the on-hand balance in your checking account, while credit card spending is limited to your credit limit.

The primary purpose of credit cards is to provide financial protection that isn't easily available from other sources. The credit card company serves as a middleman if you have a dispute with a merchant. They can be used as a ready source of emergency funds if your car breaks down in an out-of-the- way place. And they are essential if you want to secure a purchase that you're trying to make on the Internet or telephone (e.g., airline tickets, hotel room). Credit cards are therefore ideally suited for making short-term purchases (i.e., purchases that you can pay off in one to two months). Long-term debts do not belong on your credit card. The different types of credit cards are summarized as follows:

Debit cards extract the money for whatever you just purchased from your checking or savings account.

Gold and platinum cards offer preferential services like product warranties and theft insurance.

Reward cards offer you an incentive for their use at a discount at specified retail outlets.

Affiliate cards like Amazon's Visa Card offers discounts off their Internet product line.

Charge cards like American Express work like a credit card but require the balance to be paid off monthly.

Specialty cards are typically issued by department stores and oil companies.

There are several different structures used by credit card companies for the fees they charge. Some have lower interest rates but charge an annual fee. Other varieties offer competitive interest rates but vary in their bonus features. One way to find out all the options and possibly the best one for you is to visit *www.e-wisdom.com*. This website offers personalized recommendations based on information you supply and shows comparison charts so that you can see the differences between all the cards offered. You may also choose to look at *www.card ratings.com,* which offers a variety of resources to help you understand everything related to credit cards.

Controlling Plastic

People get into trouble using credit cards because it's too easy! All you have to do is pull that magic plastic card out of your wallet, hand it to the cashier, and with one swipe you become the instant owner of something. You don't even have to think about how you're going to pay for it until you get your credit card statement in another month. Your initial shock at the total balance that's due on the statement turns into a smile when you look at the small minimum payment due. Getting too many credit cards and chasing lower interest rates by transferring balances from card to card compounds the credit card debt problem. Many people become focused on the rate rather than the balance.

If you're charging everything to your credit cards, how do I just kick the habit for good? Kicking the credit card habit is a lot like kicking cigarettes. Hiding them in a safe place won't cut it. Take all of the credit cards out of your wallet, stack them neatly in a pile, and cut up all of them except for one to be used for emergencies only. If you are not able to accomplish this first step, you will never cure your credit card habit. Replace your credit cards with a debit card. If you don't have a debit card, visit the bank where you have a checking account and they will give you one. Start paying with either a debit card or check. Tell your family and close associates what you are doing and solicit their advice and encouragement.

The first step is to determine what your personal credit limit should be by figuring out how much you can afford to pay each month for credit purchases. Once you establish your personal credit limit, plan your credit spending so that your total payments cover, at a minimum, your credit purchases plus interest. Record everything you charge in a memo book so you know where you are at any time during the month. You may be able to do this step online by viewing your account activities on your card's website. Pay off the balance that is closest to its limit. If your card is maxed out, lenders can use that as an excuse to raise your interest rate. Paying off these high-balance cards can help you improve your credit score and ultimately reduce your total interest costs. So it's up to you to establish the credit limit that you can realistically handle.

Pay off the smallest balance first. This approach quickly rewards you with achieving a zero balance on at least one of your accounts, a victory that will encourage you to continue your pay off plan. But if your other card debts are accruing at higher interest rates, you could end up paying more in total interest. Pay off the cards with the highest rates first. This is perhaps the most practical plan since it is designed to eliminate your costliest accounts first. However, it may take you longer to achieve if it has a high balance due.

As high-interest card balances get paid off, you'll end up with money you didn't know you had for investing or to pay off other loans. Finally, once you're out of debt, wonderful things will happen. You'll start buying less of what you really don't need. Yes, you may keep one or two cards for emergency expenses to cover yourself. But when you learn to consistently pay the balance off at the end of each month, you will know you've kicked the credit card habit for good. Remember for every month you miss making a minimum balance payment, thirty or more points can get deducted from your credit score.

Avoiding Foreclosure

If you are facing the possibility of a foreclosure on your home, it is important that you understand that nobody wins in a foreclosure. The homeowner gets a bad credit record and the lender wastes a lot of time and money going through the foreclosure process. That gives you a fighting chance of avoiding foreclosure. Call your lender a soon as you get a foreclosure notice. Explain why you're having difficulty making payments and what you will do to catch up to avoid foreclosure to resolve the problem. Be prepared to provide financial details of your monthly income and expenses. Options that you may want to consider are:

- Refinance even at a higher interest rate if it will lower your monthly payments.

- Ask the lender for permission to make partial payments. Some lenders will allow you to do this for a short time.

- Ask for a modification to your existing loan. Perhaps you can pay back what you owe at the same interest rate over a longer period of time to reduce your monthly payments.

Avoid get-out-of-debt schemes. The fees for get-out-of-debt loans are typically outrageous, and the loans usually just stretch out your payments, costing you much more than if you had paid off the original debt. The get-out-of-debt companies are riddled with fraud and phony come-ons that are designed to part you from whatever money you have left.

Chapter 4

Where To Find Extra Money

*If you don't turn over every rock looking for money,
you'll never find any*

It takes money to pay off and to get out of debt – something that you probably may not have after you've paid your monthly expenses. In this chapter, we point you to several places that may help you find the extra cash you need. When you hit a winner that gives you cash, the reward of knowing that you're doing something right will motivate you to continue your search.

Cut Gasoline Expenses

There are several things you can do to improve your car's miles per gallon (MPG) to reduce what you're spending for gasoline by 15 percent or more. Accelerate smoothly and avoid sudden starts, which are hard on the engine and use more gas. When braking, take your foot off the accelerator well in advance of the stop sign or light to allow gravity to slow down your car. Racing to a stop sign so that you can jam on the brakes substantially reduces your MPG and wears out the brakes. Check your owner's manual and use gasoline with the octane rating recommended by the manufacturer. Buying gas with higher octane than necessary is a waste of money.

Higher freeway speeds generally reduce MPG. Most cars get their best MPG at cruising speeds of 55 miles per hour. Anything beyond that reduces MPG. When you're cruising down a long hill or grade, take your foot off the accelerator and allow gravity to help move the car. Keep your tires inflated at the proper pressure. Underinflated tires cause excessive tire wear and waste gasoline. Don't carry unneeded weight in your car. Excess weight puts an additional load on the engine and wastes gasoline. Use your air conditioner only when it is needed. Air conditioners put an extra load on the engine and eat up extra gas. Keep your vehicle tuned. Dirty air cleaners, improper valve clearances, worn plugs, and dirty oil all contribute to poor gas mileage.

Cut Home Energy Bills

Utility bills can be a significant monthly expense. In many parts of the country, utility companies offer lower rates to customers who use their electric services during off-peak hours. Off-peak hours generally refer to hours that are outside of prime business hours when the demand for electricity is at its highest. By taking advantage of off-peak rates, you can significantly reduce your electric bill. Here are several additional ways to save on your utility bills:

Heating your home is one of your highest expenses during the winter months. Turn your heat down or off when nobody is home. Put on a sweater when you get home and turn the heat back on. Close the heat vents in any room that does not need to be heated. Make sure that pipes will not freeze in these areas, however. Use a space heater to heat the areas you use most in addition to your regular heat.

Cooling a home during the summer months is also an expensive proposition. Turn your air conditioner down or off when nobody is home, even if you leave the house for a short shopping trip. Close the AC vents in any room that does not need to be cooled. Use energy-efficient fans instead of air conditioning whenever possible.

Cut Food Costs

What are some ways to save when I shop for food? Anyone can lower grocery bills by using coupons from the Sunday paper, eating the leftovers in the refrigerator first before you go shopping, and cleaning out the pantry. But how do you establish a grocery shopping style that will allow you to consistently reduce your monthly grocery bill without sacrificing the foods your family enjoys? Here's how:

Plan your meals and reduce the temptation of going out to eat or ordering fast food. Keep your pantry and freezer stocked with good, quick-fix meals. Buy bargain-priced in-season produce and check the offer against the regular price before you assume you're getting a deal. Make a list before you head to the grocery store of everything you need and then scan the store ads to find sales on any item on your list. Don't buy non-grocery items like health or beauty products in a grocery store unless you know they are competitively priced.

Always check unit prices and container weights. Just because two identical items with different brands appear to be in the same size container does not mean that the weight of the food content is the same. Don't forget to give the cashier all of your coupons and check the register receipt to make sure you got credit for every coupon. Shop at more than one store and take advantage of their sales.

Refinance Your Home

If you're considering refinancing your home, first determine why you want to refinance (i.e., financial goal). Are you trying to lower your monthly payments? Or are you trying to pay off your home faster so that you can apply your mortgage payment to pay off other debts? Your financial goal will help determine if you should refinance and what type of loan to get. Run the numbers. Shop for mortgage refinance loans that will give you a clearer idea of how much refinancing will cost you and then use a good web refinance calculator such as *www.hsh.com/usnrcalc.htmf* to help you determine if it's worthwhile.

There are ways to reduce your monthly house payment without having to refinance. For example, if mortgage insurance is included in your monthly mortgage payment, get rid of it if you can. When you purchased your home, you may have been required to carry mortgage insurance if you put down less than a specified percent of your home's purchase price. Mortgage insurance protects your lender (not you) in the event that you default on your mortgage, and it is expensive. It can cost you as much as $50 a month for every $100,000 you borrowed. If the value of your home is now 20 percent or more above what you owe on it through what you have paid on the principle and/or appreciation, you should aggressively try to get your lender to cancel mortgage insurance. It's a rip-off that lenders and insurance companies have known about for years. Now you to know about it.

In summary, there are two general conditions you must be able to meet to drop mortgage insurance, depending on the rules of your mortgage company: (1) your mortgage balance is less than 80 percent of what you paid for the house and (2) your mortgage balance is 75 percent or less of the current appraised value. Check with your mortgage company to get the exact percentages that apply to your mortgage.

Get a Cheaper Car

What does a lender mean when they say you're "upside down" in your car loan? It means that you owe more than your car is worth, which puts you at serious financial risk. For starters, it prevents you from refinancing the loan on your car. If your car is stolen or totaled, you could find yourself owing money on a car you don't have. If for some reason you have to sell it for less than what you owe, you still have car payment debts hanging over you. There is a type of insurance called guaranteed auto protection that can cover the gap if your car gets stolen or totaled if you are upside down.

What can you comfortably afford to pay on a monthly basis for a car loan? Don't buy a car if you are upside down in your current car. Pay it off first. When you take out a loan, determine how long you plan to keep the new car and make sure the term of your loan does not exceed that or you will be upside down in the car you're buying. Know what your credit score is and what interest rate you're entitled to. Auto loans are strongly driven by scores, so make sure you don't get stuck with a more expensive loan.

Plug Insurance Leak

How can you reduce your property taxes? Find out if you qualify for any special property tax exemptions in your state. These exemptions aren't widely publicized by most states. Many states offer exemptions if you're over sixty-five, disabled, a veteran, or in other special group classifications. If you believe your home is assessed too high, document your case before you see the tax assessor. If part of your case is based on the value of comparable properties in your neighborhood, you'll need written verification of three to five comparable homes. Photographs will help strengthen your case, so include those with your documents.

Make sure you follow the appeal process of your county's government to the letter. Be polite and control your irritation whenever you talk to county officials. Mad won't cut it if you're trying to solicit their cooperation. If the county appeals board rejects your challenge, you can challenge the board in court at the state level or file your complaint with the state review board. That can be an expensive proposition that will probably require an attorney, so make sure it will be worth your time and money.

One of the best places to look for hidden money is on the itemized statement that identifies what you're paying for the deductibles on your policy. Homeowner's policies typically have a deductible amount that is associated with the theft and repair portions of the policy. A deductible of $250, $500, $1,000, or higher is quoted on the policy statement. What that means is that if you have a theft or suffer insurable damage to your home, you are responsible for paying the deductible before your insurance pays the balance. The higher the deductible, the lower the insurance premium. The same principle applies to the deductible on your auto policy, which also covers theft and damage. The deductible option can be one of the most expensive components of insurance premiums. For example, the premium difference between a $500 and $250 deductible may be $100 annually. That means if you were to increase your deductible from $250 to $500, you would save $100. You are paying $100 to insure $250, which is not a good deal. Check what your insurance deductibles are and how much you could save if you increased the amount.

Reduce Interest Rates

When you look at your monthly expenses, you will notice that many of the bills include the cost of interest (e.g., mortgages, car loans, credit cards). Call each lender and ask, "Can you lower the interest rate that I'm paying on your loan?" Some lenders are willing to refinance mortgages and car loans. With credit cards, you can transfer the balance on your current card to a cheaper card. If you tell your current card issuer that you're thinking of doing this, they may reduce your rate to avoid losing your account.

Reduce Taxes

How do you find money from tax breaks? Start by knowing what tax bracket you're in. It's a simple question, but only 4 percent of people whom we interviewed in 2010 had the right answer. And yet your tax bracket is essential because it tells you how much of any extra earnings such as raises you actually get to keep. Under the U.S. graduated tax system, as income raises, so does your tax rate. Currently, the federal tax law has five basic rates: 15 percent, 28 percent, 31 percent, 36 percent, and 39 percent. However, there are hidden phase-outs of exemptions and itemized deductions that will, over time, force you into higher tax brackets even if your income doesn't increase.

The Alternative Minimum Tax (AMT) is a federal tax that affects which tax bracket you fall into, and you need to know about it because it may affect how your taxes are calculated. AMT was created several years ago to boost the taxation of wealthy individuals who use tax shelters to legally avoid taxes. While the intentions of the tax were initially good, the rules haven't kept up with the times. Many middle-income earners now earn enough and spend enough on tax-sheltered items to qualify for AMT. AMT rules severely restrict the deductions you are allowed to take, including interest deductions on a home. If you borrow money for anything except home improvements, such as to buy a car, you can't deduct the interest.

By the time you get through paying federal, state, and local taxes, you're lucky if you get to keep sixty cents out of every dollar you make. When you are faced with that kind of tax bite, you have to take a proactive position to make sure you're taking full advantage of every legal deduction that you can. Don't over withhold. One of the biggest mistakes that taxpayers make is allowing the government to withhold more taxes than they owe. If you are getting a large tax refund every year, then you probably fall into this category. You are in effect lending the government interest-free money. Increase your exemptions to lower your payroll tax deductions if, and only if, you have the self-discipline to bank the extra money into a secured savings plan like an IRA. If you don't have the willpower to do that, then keep your deductions high even though you won't be earning any interest.

Treat tax deduction receipts as if they are money, which they are. Would you willingly take a $5 bill out of your wallet, and rip it up into small pieces, even though it's not a lot of money? That is in effect what you are doing if you forget to keep a $20 tax receipt that will be worth a $5 tax refund if you're in the 25 percent tax bracket. Record every tax deduction you come across, even the small ones, in one easy-to-find folder. Even a dollar tax deduction is worth twenty eight cents (assuming you are in the 28 percent tax bracket) and it only takes a second to deposit the receipt in a conveniently located envelope. Those nickel-and-dime receipts will add up to big bucks at tax return time. You'll also need them if you're ever audited by the IRS. For example, the money you spent for tax return software for your PC, the clothes that you donated to Goodwill, and the money you put in the collection plate at church are all tax deductible.

Most people dump all of their financial paperwork including tax deduction records into a storage box. At the end of the year, when it comes time to prepare their tax returns, they'll start rummaging through the box in the hope of finding anything that even resembles a tax deduction. There are several problems that arise from this crude procedure. First, it forces you to sort through a whole year's worth of paperwork when you should be concentrating on preparing your tax return. Second, if you are content to dump everything into a box so that you don't have to think about your tax situation until the end of the year, you will miss out on potential deductions. Here's a better approach for maintaining tax records that is more productive and saves time.

At the beginning of each month, write "TAX RECORDS FOR (MONTH & YEAR)" on an envelope. Now, as you go through the month paying tax-related bills, selling stock, or engaging in any tax-related activities (e.g., making charitable donations), insert a record of each activity into the envelope. The form of the record could simply be a receipt for the payment of your property taxes or a handwritten note recording the non-reimbursed mileage driven to a business meeting. When you get to the end of the year, you'll have all of your tax records neatly filed in twelve envelopes.

Contrary to the popular rumor, the IRS is not a money-hungry monster, ready to pounce on and devour any taxpayer it can catch. The fact of the matter is that a vast majority of taxpayers are left alone. Quite frankly, the agency has bigger fish to go after, like flagrant tax cheaters, as opposed to people who are trying to honestly pay their taxes. Even if you have someone prepare your tax return, you are still responsible for reporting your taxable income and tax deductions. If you make a mathematical error on your tax return, the IRS will correct it, and adjust your return accordingly. If you declare a "questionable" deduction that gets denied by the IRS, your return will be adjusted accordingly. Yes, you will be notified of the correction and its subsequent effect on your return. No, you will not go to jail. What the IRS does not tolerate is tax evasion.

You should start preparing your tax by starting very early! Most people approach their tax planning strategy backward. They'll sit down for a few hours once a year, sometime between January 1 and April 15, and start sifting through an old shoebox of expense records in the hope of finding some tax deductions. The problem is that by that time, it is too late to take advantage of tax-saving opportunities that have existed all year long. Financially astute people approach the task by always looking ahead, rather than behind, to plan a year-round strategy that will yield the lowest possible tax rate for them on April 15. You won't find them standing in line at the post office just before midnight waiting to mail their returns. If they have a refund due, they've filed their return the same day they received their W2 forms so that they could get their refund early and reinvest the money.

People probably experience more anxiety about taxes than they do about any other debt issue. The average American household pays 40 percent of its income in federal, state, and local taxes. Clearly, taxes are one of the biggest hurdles you'll have to overcome to achieve your financial goals. Coupled with inflation, taxes steadily eat away at your wages and investments. Reducing your tax liability can help you pay down some of your debts. In order to do that, you need to have a basic understanding of the tax laws so that you can supplement your financial plan with a well-thought-out tax plan.

Filling out a tax return is almost as bad as having to go to the dentist may be worse. You spend hours digging through and sorting your tax-deductible receipts, tediously filling out a myriad of tax forms, and when you're all done, you're still left with nagging questions: Could I somehow be paying less? Did I take every legitimate deduction that's due me? A top-notch tax accountant can save you a lot of aggravation and, in many cases, identify deductions that you have overlooked. Let's face it-they know tax laws much better than you do. They're preparing tax returns at least four months out of the year, whereas you spend a couple of days out of the year doing one return. The type of tax accountant you need will depend on the complexity of your return, where you are in your financial plan, and how much you're willing to pay.

Storefront tax preparers. These are the people who work for companies like H&R Block that maintain storefronts in mini-malls throughout the country. Most of these people are working part-time during the tax season to earn extra money. They have been trained in how to ask you the right questions and fill out tax returns.

Accountants. These are people who have a four-year college degree in accounting or an MBA in accounting. Most of them work as accountants for companies and moonlight out of their home to earn extra money during the tax season. They have an edge over storefront tax preparers since they have accounting degrees and work full-time in the accounting field.

Certified Public Accountants (CPAs). CPAs are considered the tax professionals of the industry. If you have a complex return, need tough questions answered on your current return, require year-round tax and investment planning advice, and help just in case you're audited by the IRS, then you need a CPA. And yes, they are the most expensive as well.

Always arrive prepared when you meet with your tax professional. Most of them will be charging you for their services on an hourly basis, so if you waste their time because you're not prepared, you'll pay for it. After your return has been prepared, find out what you can do to reduce your taxes next year. This may require a follow-up visit with your tax preparer after the tax season is over. Or, if you are using a seasonal accountant, ask him for his advice at the same time you're having your return prepared. Don't assume that tax preparers are experts in everything that's important to you. Do your own research and homework so that you can carry on an informed conversation about key topics. Also, keep your preparer informed about any changes in your family situation that could affect your tax status, like a divorce, new baby, or marriage. If you are considering taking a tax deduction that you think is legally borderline, give them all the facts and ask for their opinion about the risk of an audit. In other words, treat your tax professional as a strategic partner who is interested in helping you achieve your financial goals.

Chapter 5

Paying Off Debt

If you conquer your debt, you will become financially free for the rest of your life

Now that you know more about your personal debt and how you can begin to manage it intelligently with a budget, you can begin to fine-tune your get-out-of-debt game plan. Getting rid of debt takes money and in the previous chapter, you should have identified several ways to come up with some of the money you'll need. Now, what are you going to do with that money? Let's explore the idea of paying yourself first before you run out and spend it on something you don't need.

Pay Yourself First

When you get your paycheck, do you immediately deposit it so that you finally have some money in your checking account and then pay off a bunch of bills to keep creditors off your back? What you may also need is a savings account that you can count on for emergency funds. You can do this if you are willing to consistently pay yourself first, before you pay any of your creditors. Make up a savings "bill" in the form of a card or envelope labeled "Savings Bill" that you keep with your other monthly bills. When it comes time to pay the bills, make sure it's the first bill that gets paid and deposit the check you make out to yourself into your savings account.

If you discover that after you pay off all your bills you have some money left over, and then make another deposit into your savings account. Deposit any coupon refund money or rebate checks you get directly into your savings account. Find out if your employer's payroll system allows you to make direct deposits into a savings account. If it does, sign up for a direct deposit tomorrow, and in a short time, you won't even miss the money that's deducted from your paycheck.

If you get a tax refund every year, consider this option. Ask payroll to increase your personal deductions, which you are allowed to do (e.g., from one to two or three). The immediate result will be a lower income-withholding amount, resulting in a larger take-home paycheck for you. Instead of paying Uncle Sam first, you are now paying yourself first. But if you take this action, you may forfeit the tax return money you get at the end of the year.

You want the money you pay yourself place somewhere so you won't be tempted to spend it on something you don't need. You may decide to give it to your spouse or trusted friend because she has more self-control about spending money. Depositing it in an "out of the way" savings account (i.e., one that is not readily accessible) is another option. For example, you could elect to increase your payroll tax deductions, which will result in more of your income being withheld in state and federal taxes. That way you'll get a tax refund at the end of the year on money that would be difficult for you to access. The disadvantage of this system is that you won't earn any interest on the withheld money.

Should you use the money you pay yourself for savings or paying off debt first? The question to save or repay first is one that people love to debate. The savers argue that the more cash you have on hand, the better you can survive a financial emergency without running up more debt. The payers will counter argue that most people are paying much higher interest on their debt than they're able to make in savings accounts. Therefore, it makes financial sense to pay off debts first. Who's right? As you probably guessed, they're both right. Saving money is a learned art that requires a lot of discipline to make happen. We would urge you to save first, and then use a portion of what you have saved-say, 50 percent-to pay off your high interest debts.

What are some simple ways of paying yourself first? Every morning before you go to work, rummage through your wallet and see if you can find a $5 bill or at least some amount of cash. Pay yourself the first thing every morning with that. Remove the bill(s) from your wallet and hide them in an out-of-the-way place. At the end of the week, you should have $25 that you can deposit into your savings account. These examples will help you get started:

Monday: Stop buying coffee on your way to work and pay yourself with the money you would have spent.

Tuesday: Turn the air conditioner up or the heat down five degrees before you leave for work and use the money you save on your utility bill to pay yourself.

Wednesday: Commute to work with one of your associates and use the money you save on gasoline to pay yourself.

Thursday: Stop buying expensive frozen foods and use the money you save to pay yourself.

Friday: Stop going out to lunch with buddies, Take a sandwich to work instead, and pay yourself with the money saved.

If you find that as soon as you pay yourself, you unfortunately spend the money on non-debt related items. Then stop paying yourself and pay someone else you trust with your money. That could be your spouse, relative, or trusted friend. Just make sure that whomever you select knows what you're trying to accomplish. There are lots of books available at the local library that address overspending. Read them all.

Why are we making a big deal out of the pay yourself first exercises? If you can't figure out a way to pay one of the most important people you know (i.e., yourself) first, then you will have difficulty resetting your debt priorities. If this were a weight loss plan, one of your first steps would be to figure out how much weight you want to lose and by when. Perhaps your answer is ten pounds over the next two months. That means you need to lose about a pound a week. Think about your pay-yourself plan the same way. Let's suppose you need to pay back $1,000 on your credit card. If you can figure out a way of paying yourself $100 a month, you can pay off the card in ten months. Once you settle on the debt diet that is right for you, do it!

Money Saving Strategies

Unfortunately, it takes money to get out of debt-and in many cases, it takes a lot of money. The previous chapter discussed several ways you could pay yourself first to come up with some extra cash for your savings account. Most of the money-saving options that were identified were relatively easy to implement. Now it is time to address some tougher areas for you to find the additional money you may need.

Figure out a way to start spending less. It is the basic philosophy that underlies the theme of this chapter and is worth repeating. We spend money on things we need, like medical care. But we also spend money on things we want but don't need, like that fancy SUV. You can't do much about the "need" part of your spending plan, but there is a lot you can do to reduce the "want" part of your spending if you are willing to address it. Get rid of all your wants until you're debt free. Then, buy your wants with cash rather than with credit.

Although you may not buy into all of the spend less ideas covered in this chapter, if you implement just a couple, you could save $100 or more per month. And these ideas should trigger thoughts about additional ways to save money. For every idea listed, you should be able to come up with at least two or more of your own. Do whatever it takes to come up with at least $100 and then hang onto the money. Here are five sources of money to consider:

1. Charge nothing for the next thirty days and add up the interest you save.

2. Buy generic brand foods whenever possible. Shop with a list and stick to it to help you avoid impulse buying. Buy generic drugs any chance you get. Purchase only sale items.

3. Make sure your car is running as efficiently as possible by getting a tune-up, properly inflating the tires, and using the least expensive gas with the proper octane rating.

4. Stop subscribing to magazines you don't read. Rent a DVD instead of going to the movies. Look for cheap and often better entertainment options like museums, zoos, a walk in the park, or picnics with friends. Start using your local library, which is free.

5. Buy gifts that are on sale for major holidays like Christmas and birthdays. Limit your spending to a specific amount. Remember, it is the thought that counts.

We all have great stories about something that we bought used for a "fantastic" bargain price, perhaps at a garage sale. The rapid expansion of eBay attests to the national infatuation of buying used. And who can really argue the point? For example, a new Sony widescreen television that sells for $1,000 can routinely be purchased Searching for on eBay for $500 or less. Consider buying used any chance you get to save money.

Payoff Strategies

Some financial advisors will encourage you to pay-off the smaller debts first regardless of interest rates to reduce your number of debts faster. Others say you should accept a multi card balance transfer offer and start paying on the one card while you still have access to credit on the "paid off" cards. The credit card consolidation option opens you up to the temptation of adding more debt to the very cards that got you into trouble in the first place. Both approaches are wrong. However, it makes financial sense to pay off your highest interest rates first because those are the ones that are costing you the most.

In general, pay off your most expensive loans first, the ones that are charging you the highest interest rates. However, it's not a hard-and-fast rule. For example, if a lower-rate card has the highest balance and the largest monthly finance charge, you'll want to pay that down first. If you are considering paying off one of two loans where Loan A is charging you 8 percent and Loan B is charging you 10 percent, it makes sense to pay off Loan B. But what if the interest that you're paying on Loan B is tax deductible (i.e., for a second mortgage) and you are in the 30 percent tax bracket-is that still prudent? The after-tax interest that you are really paying for Loan B is 7 percent rather than 10 percent. In this case, it may be to your advantage to pay off Loan A. A prepayment penalty on a loan could also determine if it makes economic sense to pay it off versus another higher-interest loan with no prepayment penalty.

Organize your outstanding loans from the highest to the lowest interest rate. If possible, increase the amount of your payments against your high interest rate loans first to get them paid off. A consolidation loan may be what you need at a lower interest rate to get out from under high interest rate debt. It may be smart to take out a home equity loan at a lower interest rate to pay them off. Borrow creatively at low rates to pay off high-interest loans. Many insurance companies offer low interest rate loans to their customers who have cash value in their life insurance policies. If you have a 401(k) retirement plan, check with your employer to see if you can borrow money against your plan.

At any moment in time, someone is creating a "get out of debt" scam for people who are desperately trying to get out of debt. Deal only with known debt consolidation companies in your area. Ask for references from their clients before you make any serious commitments. If you are being asked to pay a fee to start a debt consolidation program, raise your guard. Ask what the fee covers and what happens after you pay the fee. If you don't get answers that you are completely satisfied with, take a walk. One type of pay off loan you should strike off your list is an unsecured consolidation loan. The fees and interest rates for these kinds of loans are typically outrageous. They'll just stretch out your payments; ultimately costing you much more than if you had paid off your original loans.

Credit card companies are notorious with their direct mail and e-mail campaigns that entice you to consolidate all of your credit cards under their one universal credit card. Are they a good deal? Yes, if you can in fact transfer your high interest rate cards to a lower interest rate card. However, make sure you understand what the new card is proposing to do for you. Read all of the fine print in the material that they sent to you and get the answers to the following questions:

- What lower interest rate will they charge you and for how long will it remain in effect?

- What are the annual fees and any other special fees for which you will be responsible?

- What are your credit limits and restrictions on the new card?

- When the rate the new card is offering you expires (they usually do), what interest rate will you be charged?

If you don't have the money to pay off high interest loans, try to renegotiate your current loan rates. Many banks and credit card issuers would rather lower their interest rates or cut fees than lose you as a customer. If you are paying high rates for credit cards, call each card issuer and threaten to switch over to a lower rate competitor. If they won't budge, make the switch. Fortunately, there are a number of repayment plan calculators online at websites like Qpicken.com. It offers one called the Debt Reduction Planner that is excellent. Similar tools are available in personal finance software applications for about $50 at your local computer supply store.

Using Home Equity Loans

What are home equity loans, and are they a viable source of money to pay off your debt? Equity lines of credit combine the best features of mortgage loans and revolving credit. The asset (i.e., your home) secures the loan, so interest rates are far lower than unsecured credit loans. The time periods of equity loans are defined but are usually long term, like five to ten years, with regular payment periods. Interest is usually tax deductible. Equity loans can work well if the money is used to retire debt as opposed to acquiring unneeded stuff. Home equity loans, home equity lines of credit, and cash-out refinancing are the three primary ways to consolidate your debt. Here is a summary of what they are:

1. Home equity loans are fixed-rate loans. They are typically available in terms ranging from five to fifteen years. When you take out a home equity loan, you borrow the money all at once and start repaying it immediately.

2. Home equity lines of credit loans are variable-rate loans with interest rates that are tied to the prime rate with terms ranging from five to ten years. You receive a checkbook and can withdraw funds up to your credit limit and start repaying it immediately.

3. Cash-out refinancing is when you refinance your home because it has more equity in it than when you originally bought it. You are paid a lump-sum amount when the loan goes through that is the home's equity (i.e., appreciation) less any loan fees.

The mortgage loan experts will tell you to consider refinancing your mortgage when interest rates drop two percentage points below your current rate. Waiting for that kind of drop to help you lower your monthly mortgage payments could take some time. Before you pursue a refinance option, you will need to get answers to the following questions:

1. Given the current rates, how much will you save each month after you refinance?

2. How much will it cost to refinance, and will you be in your home long enough to make it worthwhile?

3. Is the term of the proposed refinance plan the same as or less than your current mortgage term?

Armed with the answers to these questions, you can quickly determine if it will be worth your while to refinance. Let's assume that it will cost you $2,000 to refinance your home, but your monthly payments will drop $100, a savings of $1,200 a year. It'll take you twenty months to break even, before the real savings begin ($2,000/$1,200 x 12 months = 20 months). If you move before the twenty months are up, you lose money by refinancing. Stay longer and you will have the advantage financially. Also keep in mind that the $1,200 a year you save is a tax deduction you can no longer take. If you're in the 25 percent tax bracket, that amounts to $300 (25% x $1,200) less that you'll get back at the end of each tax year. Therefore, your real savings may not be $1,200 a year but rather $900 ($1,200 - $300). It now takes you almost twenty-seven months ($1,200/$900 x 12 months = 27 months) to break even.

Paying Off Your Mortgage

There are several advantages to paying off your mortgage early. Doing so enables you to acquire something you care about (i.e., your home) that appreciates. It will also substantially reduce the amount of interest you'll pay over time. If you are looking to trade up to a more expensive home, nothing will get you there faster than building equity in your existing house. If you are able to pay off your mortgage before you retire, you will have a big part of your living expenses covered.

What is the primary difference between a fifteen-year and a thirty-year mortgage? Nothing can save you more money over time than paying off your home mortgage as soon as you can. Typically, people elect to take out thirty-year mortgages because it gives them plenty of time to pay off their home, while offering them lower monthly payments. However, if you can work it into your budget to have a higher monthly mortgage in order to pay off your home faster, it can dramatically improve your financial picture. If you own a home with a thirty-year mortgage, consider what a fifteen-year mortgage can do for you.

If you have a $100,000 thirty-year 7 percent mortgage, your payments are approximately $665 a month. If you finance the same amount for fifteen years, your payments would be $900 a month for a difference of only $235. You would have been able to pay off your home in half the time (fifteen instead of thirty years) and saved yourself $80,000 in interest that you can use for investments. If you can't afford the extra monthly amount required to pay your home off in fifteen years, consider making extra payments when you can to accelerate the time it takes to pay it off.

Consolidating Loans

You may be tempted to implement an instant solution to your immediate debt problem by using a home equity loan or some other type of loan to consolidate your high-interest loans into a single lower-interest loan. In some situations, consolidating loans makes sense if you have honestly addressed and resolved the basic problems that got you into debt in the first place. If you haven't done this, you could be digging yourself into a deeper debt hole. These types of loans usually turn short-term into long-term debt. So, in the long run, you could end up paying more in interest.

Consolidating your debts means taking two or more debts and rolling them up into a single lump sum debt that's hopefully at a lower interest rate with favorable terms. Unfortunately, some people use it as a convenient way of wiping out the balances of a bunch of credit cards so that they can begin using them again. That can be very dangerous to their overall debt situation. They're not just right back where they started from; they are worse off because they now have to pay back both loans. Don't let that happen to you if you decide to consolidate your debts.

How should the interest rates that I'm paying on my debts affect my decision to consolidate? Let's say you are carrying $10,000 in credit card debts at 18 percent. If you decide to pay $150 each month to pay them off, it will take you twenty-four years. If you were able to get a consolidation loan for, say, 6 percent and continued to pay $150 a month, you would pay your cards off in eight years. That is one of the main reasons why a well-thought-out and executed debt consolidation plan at the right interest rate may help you get out of debt.

66

If you decide to consolidate your debt, you need to assure yourself that you will not use consolidation as a way to run up more debt. Make sure you are prepared to get rid of all but one or two low-rate credit cards. Take those credit cards out of your wallet and replace them with a debit card. Store them in an out-of-the-way place and only use them for legitimate financial emergencies. Start paying cash for everything. If you can't pay cash, you should have a good reason, such as your car breaks down. Use a debit card instead of a credit card whenever you can.

Actively solicit the help and advice of your family and friends with regard to what you are trying to accomplish with your consolidation plan. For example, after you have shown them your plan, solicit their advice and be accountable to them to help you stay on track.

Chapter 6

Car Buying Tactics

A car can destroy you financially if you let it drive you into debt

Next to the overuse of credit cards, the automobile is the biggest cause of people falling into debt. The actual cost of a car and subsequent car payments is just the tip of the iceberg. License fees, insurance, and maintenance can easily cost several hundred dollars a month. A trip to the gas station that used to cost $50 for a tank of gas has more than doubled. If you are supporting two cars, try to get by on one. If you have a relatively new car, you would be better off with a cheaper used car that gets better mileage.

A car is one of the most expensive purchases you'll ever make. And, unlike your home, a car typically does not appreciate in value. Before you set out to buy a car, decide what kind of vehicle you will need, what options you must have, and what payments you can afford. How will you use the vehicle? Does the purchase of a new car fit into your budget and financial plan at this time? Should you consider buying a used car? Maybe you should lease one? These are just some of the questions addressed in this chapter.

Tactical Questions to Ask

There are several questions to ask yourself and anybody else in the family who will be driving the car. What kind of transportation do you need? If you travel a lot, you'll probably want a large interior and a smooth-riding car. Will the car be used primarily for commuting to work? Will it be sitting out in the sun all day while you're at work? Is fuel economy important to you? How many miles do you drive a year? What will you spend on gasoline per year if you buy a gas-guzzler versus a fuel-efficient car?

If you're thinking about a four-wheel-drive vehicle, will you really use that option? Over 80 percent of four-wheel-drive vehicle owners will never use this expensive option. How much more will four-wheel-drive cost, and is it worth the extra money? What price are you willing to pay for the car you want and what monthly payments can you afford? How long are you willing to finance the vehicle? What will it really cost you to run this vehicle annually? Don't just think in terms of gas and oil. Can you afford to maintain the type of vehicle that you want? Check the Consumer Reports guides to find out what the maintenance history is on the type of cars you're considering.

What Car Ownership Cost

When a friend asks "How much did your car cost?" you can either tell her what you paid for the thing or tell her what the real cost will be. If you just bought a $25,000 vehicle and are planning on keeping it for five years, your real cost of owning the car will be more than double that amount, or $69,250 to be precise. Using national cost averages collected by the American Automobile Association, here is how that staggering figure was calculated:

Initial cost of vehicle $25,000
State sales and other taxes (5%) $1,250
Acquisition fees (dealer fees, title, etc.) $500
Auto insurance $5,000
Total interest on auto loan or lease at 10% $5,000
State license fees over 5 years $3,000
Operating and maintenance expense $6,250
Gas @15,000 miles per year/$2.75 a gallon/25 MPG $8,250
Depreciation $15,000

Total Operating Cost Over 5 Years = $69,250

If you need additional information or help in determining the cost of owning a car, buy a copy of *The Complete Car Cost Guide* that is published by Intellichoice. Edmunds car-buying guides are available on the *www.edmunds.com.* Edmunds has long been considered one of the best resources for its outstanding reviews of new and used vehicles.

Getting Rid of Old Reliable

If you've decided to get rid of your current vehicle, one of the nagging questions in your mind is how you will dispose of Old Faithful. You can sell it to a private party or dealer, trade it in for another car, or donate it to a charity and take the tax deduction. What's your asking price and the lowest offer you'll accept? If you want a premium price, then why does it deserve that higher price? Low mileage definitely deserves a higher price. Add at least 10 percent to 15 percent to your price so that you have room to negotiate. The Kelley Blue Book provides pricing information on new and used vehicles. It's available in most major bookstores, or you can visit their web site at *www.kbb.com*.

If you're thinking about trading it in to a dealer for another car, you'll be lucky to get Kelley's Blue Book wholesale price for it. Dealers can buy cars just like yours at wholesale auctions any time they want, so don't expect them to give you a premium for your "one-of-a-kind" jewel. You are usually better off selling it on your own rather than trading it in. Whichever way you decide to go, wash and polish everything including the tires. Nothing will turn off a buyer faster than a car that looks like the inside of a garbage can, so clean everything, including the interior.

Financing a Car

Don't finance a car for longer than you expect to keep it. If you plan to keep it for four years, take out a four-year loan or better yet, take out a three-year loan. You'll save on interest payments and won't be "upside down" in the car, the industry's term for owing more on the car than it's worth if and when you trade it in. Watch out for up-front fees that some lenders add to raise the cost of their loans.

Credit union loans. If you belong to a credit union, these loans are sometimes hard to beat. The amount of money that you have for the down payment can dramatically affect the interest rate that you'll pay. You'll pay a premium if you have less than 20 percent down and many lenders won't even talk to you unless you have at least that.

Dealer financing. The best time to finance a new car is when dealers are advertising finance rates that are significantly below the market rates. Their very best rates usually carry a short repayment term like two years, so you'll need a good payment-free trade or lots of money for the down payment.

Bank financing. You won't get the title to the car until the loan is paid off, and you will be required to carry collision and comprehensive insurance with perhaps lower deductibles than what you normally carry. The best type of a bank loan to get is a simple interest loan with no prepayment penalties.

If your monthly car payment is a killer, what can I do to bring it down to earth? Most people don't know that it is easier to refinance a car loan than it is to refinance a home and, there are several advantages. There are no appraisal fees, and finance fees are usually minimal. If this option interests you, make sure you first know what your car is worth by consulting the Kelly Blue Book at *www.kbb.com.* If it is worth more than you owe, you are in good shape. If it is not, then the only option you have is asking your lender if they will either reduce the interest rate or extend the payment terms. If you have equity in your car, shop around for a better loan. The best car loans are usually offered by credit unions and online lenders. Bankrate.com is an excellent site with a search engine that can find the best rates nationally and in your area.

Leasing a Car

When you lease, you are actually renting a car for a specified period of time. Because you don't own it, you are obligated under a lease contract to maintain the vehicle and drive it a limited number of miles per year. If you try to get out of a lease before it expires, you will be required to pay significant penalties. Lease payments are not based on the total value of the car, but rather on the depreciation during the time you lease the vehicle. That's why your monthly payments are typically lower than what they would be if you financed the car for the same period as a purchase. This is one of the reasons why the popularity of leases has increased to about one-third of all new car transactions. That doesn't necessarily mean that leasing makes sense for you. Take a moment and answer the following questions to determine if leasing is right for you:

1. Do you typically trade in a new car every four years or less?

2. Do you, on average, drive less than 15,000 miles a year?

3. Do you keep your vehicle in good condition and follow routine maintenance schedules?

4. Are you self-employed and can you deduct all or part of the lease from your tax return?

5. Do you want a new car every few years for whatever reason?

If you answered yes to three or more of those questions, then you may want to consider leasing.

Buying New Versus Used

If you're thinking about buying a new car, brace yourself for one of the most challenging consumer experiences you will ever have. The new car purchasing process puts you on a playing field pitted against well-trained and intelligent salespeople. Before you go car shopping, stop by your local library and check out the recent copy of Consumer Reports' *New Car Buying Guide,* which features information on the performance and maintenance records of the major models. It's important to know how new cars are priced when you start shopping so that you can negotiate the best deal. Here's how new cars are priced.

Manufacturer's suggested retail price (MSRP) is the suggested price that is provided by auto manufacturers for cars. It's their way of assuring that all of their dealers are using standard pricing. The sticker price is the total amount that appears in the car's window. Federal law requires all new car dealers to post the base price of the car along with the cost of the options that are installed on the car. The factory invoice price seldom appears on the car window. It is usually hidden in the sales manager's file drawer. In theory, the invoice price is what the dealer paid the manufacturer for the car. Visit *www.autosite.com* if you want to find dealer invoice prices or find out about the maintenance records on cars that interest you. For a comprehensive car-buying guide, go to *www.edmunds.com*.

Although owning a new car is nice, there are many reasons to buy a good used car including the fact that they're cheaper. Registration, license fees, and insurance premiums are usually much lower for used cars. When you buy used, you don't have to pay destination charges, dealer preparation fees, and shipping charges that go along with buying a new car. According to Consumer Reports, a new car depreciates 20 percent to 30 percent the moment you drive it off the lot. You don't have that problem when you buy used. A well-built and maintained car will continue to run past 150,000 miles before it needs major engine work.

Usedcars.com provides information about buying used cars. Other sites include *www.cars.com* and *www.autotrader.com.*These site feature classified ads by Zip Code and includes links to other websites including manufacturers, dealers, auto parts stores, and accessories. As well, check out Auto Trader Online *(www.traderonline.com),* Kelley Blue Book's Classifieds *(www.kbb.com),* or Online Auto *(www.onlineauto.com).* or Auto Web Interactive *(www.autoweb.com).*

Maintenance Options

Finding a good automotive repair facility can be challenging and frustrating at the same time, particularly if you've just run into

Dealerships. Most car buyers tend to use the dealership's service department when their car is still under warranty. The dealers like that because they want you to return for another new car when you're ready, and, of course, they also want your very profitable service business. They are more expensive but guarantee their work.

National chains. National chains like Midas and Firestone are generally less expensive than dealerships. Many are franchise operations so you could be dealing with a national chain that's owned locally. Most of them offer a wide range of repair services and guarantee their work.

Independent shops. A good independent shop can be your best option. You can usually communicate directly with the owner or head technician who, over time, gets to know your car. If you are an AAA member, the association can provide you with a list of approved facilities as well a rough estimate of costs (i.e., high, medium, or low).

Inner Auto Parts offers an online service (*www.innerauto.com*) where you can find lots of information like how to choose a mechanic and how to maintain your transmission and engine. Theautoshop.com also offers helpful advice and information. Consumer Reports (*www.consumerreports.com*) offers helpful information on warranties as well as the maintenance and service statistics for new and used cars.

Insurance Options

Heightened competition among auto insurers, coupled with safer driving and fewer claims, has kept auto insurance rates from going through the roof. However, the fact remains that your auto insurance probably is the highest monthly premium you're paying on any of your insurance policies. Don't over insure. Most states require a minimum amount of liability insurance, but the other types of coverage are usually optional. You may not need collision and comprehensive coverage on an older car if its value is less than ten times the annual premium. Consider raising your deductible for comprehensive and collision. Going from a $250 deductible to $500 or even $1,000 can reduce your insurance cost by 15 percent to 20 percent annually.

Take advantage of discounts if you drive less than the average number of miles per year, install an alarm system, get married, or are over a certain age. There are a number of websites on the Internet to help you compare rates. Progressive Insurance's site (*www.progressive.com*) will offer you a company quote and up to three quotes from major insurers. Quicken at *quicken.intuit.com* offers online quotes plus e-mailed bids from insurers.

Chapter 7

Home Buying Tactics

If you're winning the debt game, buying a home could be a smart strategy

We all want to stay ahead in the staying out of debt game. Debt is a tough opponent to play and it has beaten more good people than we will ever know about. If you are not yet out of debt, but you were able to free up some cash and put it where it will do you the most good, then you are winning the game, but you're still in it. Just remember that managing your money is an ongoing necessity to achieve your goals. If you continue to make good financial decisions, and develop good spending, saving, and investment habits, you will be the ultimate winner. In this chapter, we will discuss where buying a home fits into your overall financial and retirement strategy.

Renting Versus Owning

Should you rent instead of buying a home? The answer to that depends on your personal situation, but here are some things to think about. To help you get started, go to *www.wellsfargo.com/challenge*. Wells Fargo has an extensive site about home buying, including workshops and seminars for the prospective home buyer. If you decide to rent, understand that you are paying someone else's mortgage and helping them experience the appreciation and tax advantages of owning property. However, renting is sometimes advantageous when you move to a new area and are not sure where you want to live, or you decide to build a house and need temporary shelter during the process. Don't rule out renting because it really depends on your situation and needs. Weigh the pros and cons of owning versus renting to determine which solution works best for you.

Can You Afford One?

To help answer that question, put yourself through a trial test by renting for several months. If you pay $1,000 a month in rent, can you save $400 (40 percent) a month to cover the extra expenses associated with home ownership? If not, then you are not ready to purchase a home.

If routine home maintenance tasks like mowing the yard are not something that you want to do, you may want to consider buying a condominium. Condominiums are homes that are attached to one another thereby sharing common walls. You own a unit and share common grounds such as recreational areas with the other condominium owners through what is called a homeowners' association. One of the major advantages condominiums have over freestanding houses are that they generally cost less to buy and require less upkeep. Each owner pays a monthly maintenance fee to the homeowners' association to maintain the exterior walls of each condominium and to provide landscaping services. You do not own the land under the unit-that's owned by the association.

Single-family homes generally have a greater potential for capital appreciation than condominiums if they're located in an area where property values have consistently risen over the past several years. Quite often, small investments in cosmetics such as paint and landscaping can substantially improve their selling price. They offer more privacy than what you will find in a condominium since you are not sharing a common wall with your neighbor. However, since you are responsible for all maintenance work, you can expect to spend more to maintain a home than you would a condominium. You own the land under and around your home.

Why Buy a Home?

Buying a home is an investment subject that deserves special consideration because it can work for you during all the ups and downs of the economic cycle. During inflationary periods, home values typically go up at rates that beat the inflation. And when a recession hits, you still benefit from one of the best tax shelters there is. During much of the 1990s, real estate was almost a "can't lose" investment. Cooling markets in many areas of the country in 2008 combined with more stringent home mortgage qualification standards have made home investments somewhat less alluring, at least in the short term. Yet a home remains a worthwhile component in a well-balanced financial plan and, if chosen properly, will reward you with a consistent rate of return that will do quite well during inflationary periods.

The basic home is still one of the best real estate investments you can make. It's also a great tax shelter, and if you work it right, a home that is paid for when you retire can become the anchor of your retirement plan. Some would argue that the appreciation of private homes has lagged behind Standard & Poor's stock market average over the past ten years. However, their numbers can be deceiving. Let's suppose you bought a $100,000 home and invested $100,000 into the stock exchange ten years ago. Over that period of time, the average annual appreciation of your home would have been 6 percent, while you would have enjoyed a 13 percent average annual appreciation on your stocks.

This scenario should also ask the question "Why would you have wanted to invest in a home instead of the stock market ten years ago?" When you bought the house in this scenario, let's assume that you were able to negotiate a $100,000 mortgage with a 20 percent ($20,000) down payment. This was not the case when you bought $100,000 in stock. You had to come up with $100,000 out of your personal account to make the trade because it's illegal to borrow money to buy stocks. Here's the revised bottom line at the end of ten years. Your house would have been worth approximately $185,000, or $85,000 more than you paid for it, based on an initial investment of$20,000.

Your stock would have more than doubled over the same period to approximately $210,000, or $110,000 more on your initial investment of $100,000. Yes, you doubled your money in the stock market, but you made over four times the $20,000 you initially invested in your home ($85,000/$20,000 = 4.25).

Cost of Owning a Home

Keep in mind that it is really not the price of the home that you can afford but rather the mortgage you can afford. As a general rule, your mortgage payment including property taxes and insurance should not exceed 25 percent of your disposable income. The type of home you should buy is of course a matter of personal preference. Newer or new homes can offer you incentives to lower mortgage costs and down payments. New homes are covered under warranty for a period of time, which allows you to not spend money on remodeling and maintenance. If you're not concerned about the price of gasoline, you may be able to afford more house if you are willing to drive farther to commute to work.

There are extra expenses to consider when figuring your budget for a home purchase versus renting. You will pay property taxes, which could vary from 1 percent to 3 percent of your home's value. You will need to protect your investment with homeowners insurance, which can add $25 a month expense per $100,000 of valuation. If you are unable to come up with a 20 percent down payment, which most financial institutions require, you may have to pay private mortgage insurance on the part of the loan that covers the 20 percent down payment. This is to protect the financial institution from risks and can cost as much as $40 a month per $100,000 of your mortgage. Also, factor in monthly repairs and maintenance expenses into your budget.

Finding Bargains

Before you go out with a realtor to shop for a home, you need to do some preliminary homework on pricing. One way to do this is to look at open houses in the area you are interested in. Keep track of what real estate is doing in your area of interest while you are renting and saving for your down payment. Your local paper should have, by Zip Codes, the recent average sales prices of homes and condos in your target area. You can start your own housing spreadsheet to assess what the values are so that when you are ready to buy, you do not overpay. How long are homes sitting on the market in your target area? Are they selling above or below the listing prices? If homes are selling within ninety days and are at or close to full list price, you are at a disadvantage as a buyer because it is a "sellers' market." However, if homes are lingering for months on the market and selling way below their asking price, congratulations. You are in a "buyers' market" and that is to your advantage.

Microsoft's real estate website (*www.realestate.msn.com*) covers every step of the buying process from researching neighborhoods to applying for a mortgage. The site also allows you to visit over 500,000 listings throughout the country. Consider buying a fixer-upper if you are handy with tools and paintbrushes. A structurally sound house that is priced 20 percent to 30 percent below market because it needs some "tender loving care" could be a good investment. To make sure we are all on the same page, tender loving care means a home needs cosmetic care and not expensive structural repairs like replacing a cracked slab. Look for distress situations where a seller has to put a house on the market for a quick sale because of a job transfer, a divorce settlement, or to settle an estate.

Never be afraid to submit an offer that is substantially less than the asking price. If your realtor balks at submitting your low price offer, get another one. If you can, buy the cheapest house in the neighborhood. The higher-priced homes will tend to pull the value of yours up as they appreciate. If you are at the higher-price end of the neighborhood, you'll restrict your buying opportunities when you sell. Some people like to buy down rather than buy up! Also, you may want to consider buying a home that is in foreclosure where the owners have turned their property over to the lender. Foreclosures have reached their highest level in years and lenders are often anxious to resell their foreclosures to qualified buyers at discount rates.

Thoroughly inspect any home you're thinking about buying. Read books that show you how to conduct your own home inspection and consult with knowledgeable friends who can help you determine if the house is in good shape. Consider hiring a professional home inspector to conduct a survey for you. Let your fingers do the walking through the Yellow Pages to find one. Many states require home inspectors to be licensed. Ask the seller to include a home warranty in the selling price when you submit an offer. A typical warranty covers major home systems like plumbing, heating, and electrical equipment. Home warranties also protect the seller from possible legal action resulting from their failure to disclose known defects in the house before it was sold. Lower your consumer debt so that you'll have a better chance to qualify for a higher loan. Even if your mortgage rate and payments are higher than what you wanted, you can always refinance or prepay the loan down.

Home Mortgages

Most homes are financed with a loan secured by a deed of trust, commonly referred to as a mortgage. Mortgages are available from many sources, including commercial banks, savings and loan associations, credit unions, insurance companies, and mortgage companies. Most lenders offer fully amortized loans in which you repay the principle (borrowed amount) and the interest over a specified period of time. At first, most of your payment goes toward the interest.

As you continue to make payments over time, an increasing part of your payment goes to pay off the principle and a decreasing part goes to interest. The interest on most loans is classified as either fixed-rate or variable-rate. In fixed-rate loans, the interest rate and your monthly payments remain the same over the term of the loan, which is usually fifteen or thirty years. Variable-rate loans offer an interest rate that fluctuates with the market interest rate. They are usually indexed to the "prime rate" plus points. The prime rate is the preferred interest rate that is offered by lending institutions to their best corporate customers. The prime rate will fluctuate up or down at any point in time with changes in the economy. A point is equivalent to one interest point, so if a bank offers you a variable-rate mortgage at prime plus two points, and prime is at 6 percent, you'll pay 8 percent interest.

How does your credit rating affect mortgage rates? Your FICO score will be a major factor in determining the interest rate you'll pay for a home mortgage. In general, the lower your score, the higher the interest rate you'll be charged. The following table will give you an idea of how higher interest rates affect your mortgage.

Monthly Mortgage Costs

4%	$477	$955	$1,432
5%	$537	$1,074	$1,610
6%	$600	$1,200	$1,800
7%	$665	$1,330	$1,995
8%	$734	$1,467	$2,310

An increasing number of savvy home buyers are seeking home loans on the Internet. Over a billion dollars in home loans are already flowing through Internet channels. There are several home mortgage sites on the Internet that offer different levels of service. Here are a few of the better sites to check:

E-Loan at *www.eloan.com.* E-Loan offers mortgages from sixty lenders to home buyers in thirty-nine states. They will handle the entire transaction online and with Federal Express for document delivery.

Home Shark at *www.homeshark.com.* Home Shark offers a service that is similar to E- Loan. They represent several lenders that operate out of forty-six states. You can also search their home sellers' database of 1 million homes nationwide.

MSN Real Estate at *www.realestate.msn.com.* This is Microsoft's mortgage service, which is similar to Intuit's service. Its aim is to become an overall home-buying service.

Quicken at *www.quickenmortgage.com.* Intuit offers a service that lets you compare rates and terms with eleven national lenders. If you select one of the lenders, you work with that lender to close the loan.

Chapter 8

Making Hard Choices

There is no easy way out of debt and the longer you wait, the harder it becomes

Sometimes cutting back on what you're spending for discretionary items is all you need to do to get your financial life in order. If that doesn't make a big enough dent to help you make ends meet, you may need to look at some major items that are costing you the most money. You may have to make some hard choices now if you truly want to become debt free and financially independent. If you haven't been able to bring your expenses in line with what you make, the question is not whether you are going to have to make hard choices, but rather which hard choices you are going to take.

Hard Choice Basics

Who should you see who can help me decide what hard choices you need to make? In the end, you probably are the one who will have to make final decisions about what you need to do to resolve your debt problems. However, that should not stop you from seeking the advice of anyone you can find who may have some viable ideas that may help. Immediate sources to consider are any and all family members who will be directly affected by any hard choice you're considering. Ask personal friends and associates whom you can trust not to disclose your personal situation to others and who have personal finance expertise for advice. Show whomever you're talking to a list of the choices you are considering and ask them for their opinion. Then sit back and listen to what she has to say.

Changing Your Lifestyle

If your personal debt is escalating to the point where you can't even pay the minimum on your debts and collection agencies are hounding you, then you need to take some hard action right now. Consider cutting back on what you're paying for rent or mortgage payments until you get my debt under control? Will that necessitate a move? If car expenses including the high price of gasoline are taking every spare dime you have, consider getting rid of it and start using public transportation. If the interest rates that you're paying on credit cards is exorbitant, get rid of them. If you can't save enough money to cover purchases so you just go deeper into debt, you may have to declare bankruptcy. Less drastic option to consider are summarized as follows:

Your Car: Is your car sabotaging your ability to make ends meet? Is there a cheaper way for you to get back and forth to work each day? There probably is if you think about it. If you're willing to get rid of your car for a while, you could save the cost of its payments, upkeep, gasoline, and insurance. If you can't survive without a car, how about trading your car for a less expensive model that can get you from point A to point B just fine, with less luxury. This will also save you money on auto insurance. If you have an older car, you may not need expensive collision coverage.

Your Home: Should you consider selling your home? Unfortunately, it may be that selling your home is a solution to your debt problem that you have to consider. It may be necessary to swap a larger house for a smaller, more affordable one, or rent for a while. If you're already renting, can you find a cheaper place to rent? Can you keep the cost of moving in line with what you will be saving? Would moving closer to work be more cost effective (i.e., cut transportation costs)?

Credit Cards: Should you consider getting rid of all your credit cards? Yes. The average credit card carries an interest rate of 18 percent or more. If you are making the minimum payment allowed on a credit card with a $1,000 balance, it will take you twelve years to pay it off. You might say, "How can I survive without my credit cards?" It's a big change, but you can do it. You don't need to close all your accounts. Leave one open in case you need to use it for emergency funds.

Saving Money: Are you not able to save any money? How can you change your ways? By not saving, you are forced to borrow anytime you need something that you didn't plan for. The itemized statement that you receive from your credit card company is probably loaded with unplanned items that you purchased last month. If your car broke down, you probably borrowed the money to get it repaired. And the list goes on. If you don't have a savings account, you are going to put everything on your credit card, which increases your debt load. One of the most basic decisions you need to make is to open a savings account. That will take about ten minutes the next time you're at the bank. Now comes the hard part. Start depositing a set amount every month into your savings account, and at the end of three months, see if all the money you deposited is still in your savings. If it is, you are on your way to saving money. If it's not, you are back where you started from.

Selling Stuff: If you own some assets that you don't need or want, how can you determine what to sell them for? Whatever item you are considering selling, it is important to have an idea of its value before you sell it. If it's a motor vehicle, consult a guidebook like the Kelley Blue Book *(www.kbb.com)*. If it's a piece of jewelry, get it appraised by a certified appraiser. If you are selling a household item that would be difficult to get an appraisal on, see what similar items are selling for in the classified advertisements or on *www.ebay.com*. Decide whether you want to sell your item yourself or through a broker. There are brokers listed online who are willing to sell just about anything for a fee.

Living a frugal or even a goal-oriented life is difficult in America, where every time you turn around, advertisers are encouraging you to spend more. It may be helpful to you to find others or a group in your area who share your get-out-of-debt goals. A good place to start your search on the Internet is at *www.simpleliving.net.* You might want to also investigate Debtors Anonymous *(www.debtorsanonymous.org)*, which is a twelve-step program designed to help people kick their addiction to overspending. The site also includes invaluable information about ways to save money.

Financial Emergencies

You need separate funds to cover financial emergencies. The emergency fund is the most important savings category that you can have. It is created to cover expenses related to emergencies such as the loss of a job, unexpected medical expenses, car repairs, or other crisis situations that cost money. It should be an important part of your financial plan because the last thing you want is to be forced to go back into debt to cover emergency expenses. How much you need in emergency reserves depends on you. A minimum of three months' salary is recommended. Set a monetary target and begin making deposits into a separate savings account for this purpose. Short-term savings funds are used for planned expenses and emergency expenses. Regular recurring contributions are essential to assure that your "nest egg" builds at a consistent rate. Long-term savings are typically invested in equities that can provide long-term growth.

Fighting Off Bankruptcy

Should you consider bankruptcy to get out of debt, or are there alternatives? There are alternatives to bankruptcy. Lenders may be willing to compromise their claim for a smaller cash payment or they may be willing to stretch payments out so you can pay their debts off over a longer period of time. You won't know what they are willing to do unless you make the contact. It costs you nothing to ask, and always remember that the last thing creditors want to do is to turn you over to a collection agency. They'll only get about half of whatever the agency collects. When *Smart Money* magazine called ten of the largest credit card issuers, posing as a distraught debtor, five agreed to reduce their interest rates.

However, an increasing number of people have run up six figure debt on five figure incomes. These people will never obtain an income level that will allow them to get out of debt. They are more likely to struggle for years trying to manage their personal finances and will never be able to pay off what they owe. The huge interest rates they're saddled with will compound the financial burden they are under as time goes on. If in your judgment there is no possibility of your getting out of debt, then you need to consider the option of bankruptcy. If you need more information about bankruptcy, go to the website at *www.clearbankruptcy.com.*

If you declare bankruptcy, you file by drawing up a plan to repay your existing debts, usually within a three-year period. Depending on your circumstances, your plan could show how you'll pay off your debts in full, or in part, where you pay only a percentage of every dollar you owe. When you file, the court issues a restraining order stopping your creditors' collection efforts. If the court approves your payment plan, you'll make a single monthly payment to a court-appointed trustee who in turn pays your creditors. As long as you are under the plan, the court can exercise some control over your finances. For example, if you take on new debt, the court can immediately cancel the plan.

How much does it cost to declare bankruptcy? Most bankruptcies are performed using the services of an attorney. When you call a bankruptcy attorney, ask what the minimum charge is for a private individual's bankruptcy. If they tell you, "Well, that all depends," politely end the conversation and call the next attorney on your list. There are two points that we want to make here. First, bankruptcy is not a complicated legal procedure, so it is not unreasonable to ask for basic cost information. Second, attorney fees for bankruptcies can vary, so it pays to shop. It is possible for you to represent yourself in bankruptcy. If this approach interests you, get a how-to book on bankruptcy.

The act of declaring bankruptcy is not something you want to openly share with anyone you don't trust. It should initially be shared with the people who are directly affected by the act of declaring bankruptcy. That includes your spouse, whose credit rating will be severely damaged just like yours. The only other people on your immediate list would be those who need to know what you are doing. If you decide to discuss the matter with a "don't need to know" person, make sure you have a good reason for doing so. For example, if this person can provide you with some information critical to making the decision, then contact him.

Leveraging Your Home Equity

Home equity is the difference between what your home is worth on the open market and what you owe on it. You don't want to squander a loan on a long-term asset to accommodate short-term spending. Using your home equity for items like vacations, big screen TVs, and credit card payments is foolish. The intent of this chapter is to give you a better appreciation for what home equity is and why it is an essential part of your financial well-being.

Who makes home equity loans, and what are the costs and risks? Savings and loan associations and banks are the primary sources for home equity loans. You typically can get a lower interest rate on an equity loan than you can on just about any other loan. Home equity loans are not inexpensive to set up, however. In most cases, you will be charged an appraisal fee for your home and loan origination fees that will cost you several hundred dollars. Make sure these fees are disclosed to you before you enter into any loan agreement. Equity loans are typically from five to fifteen years in duration and therefore require a higher monthly payment than a thirty-year mortgage.

Be aware that by borrowing against the equity in your home, you may be leveraging the most valuable asset you have in your portfolio. The risks can therefore be significant. Using up all the equity in your home in a fast-rising real estate market poses several problems, as we recently witnessed in the subprime fiasco. Hot markets can suddenly cool, dropping the average home value. If you have used up all of the equity and need to relocate, you may be forced to sell your home for less than what you owe on it. And if you fail to make your equity loan payments, the lending institution can foreclose on your home.

When does it make sense to consider a home equity loan? A home is a source of wealth for many people, and its equity should not be used on something that is of a lesser value, like a luxury car. NEVER use home equity to cover expenses like vacations or weddings, or for buying big-ticket items like a new car that you want but don't need. Using the equity in your home to pay off high interest debts may make sense if you have proven to yourself that you will not run up more debt once your old debt is paid off. There are advantages to using home equity financing to pay off other debts.

1. Interest rates: They are often much lower than debt rates and the interest on an equity loan is tax deductible.

2. Forced savings: Instead of paying rent that goes nowhere, you are paying into a home that you will someday own.

3. Tax deductions: The interest on your mortgage and property taxes is one of the few remaining tax shelters for most people.

If you are late in your payments or fail to make an equity loan payment, your lender has the legal right to foreclose on your home. Miss one payment and you will receive by certified mail a "breach letter" from your lender advising you of your contract violation. You will be given thirty days to respond. If you don't respond, that letter serves as the right of the lender to foreclose and take over ownership of your home. Do not even think about taking out a home equity loan if there is any doubt in your mind that you won't be able to pay it back.

Selling Your Home

Although many of us stepped into our homes deep in debt years ago, thanks to inflation, we've ended up with an asset that's worth a lot more than what we paid for it. Over the last three decades, the rise in single-family home prices has become the cornerstone of affluence for many Americans. The opportunity to leverage the equity they've built up in their homes has become the foundation of their retirement plan. As you approach retirement, you may want to trade down and move into a smaller home. Before you do that, estimate your profit before you consider selling. What will it cost for an acceptable replacement? If the potential profit from selling your home is minimal, it might not be worth the effort of trading down. Time the sale of your home to take advantage of tax breaks.

If you or your spouse is fifty-five or older, you can exclude from taxes up to $500,000 of the capital gains on the sale of your home. If your gain exceeds $500,000 you may also be able to defer tax on the rest by reinvesting in a new residence. Check out all of the tax angles with your accountant before you sell.

Consider trading down. Estimate your profit before you consider selling. What will it cost for an acceptable replacement? If the potential profit from selling your home is minimal, it might not be worth the effort of trading down. Time the sale of your home to take advantage of tax breaks. Sell your home and move to a part of the country where the cost of housing and living are lower. Not only will you get more home for your money, you will also get the added benefit of a lower cost of living in the new area.

Reverse Mortgages

Consider keeping your home and refinancing it with an individual reverse mortgage (IRM) or a leaseback. In this arrangement, a lender receives part or all of the equity in your home, in return for payments that you receive for the rest of your life. Make sure you know the pros and cons before signing this kind of contract.

A reverse mortgage allows you to borrow back the equity in your principal residence. As you once paid the bank to build up the equity in your home, some banks are willing to repay you some of your equity and allow you to stay in your home. In most cases, you have to be sixty-two or older to qualify for a reverse mortgage. The amount that you can borrow depends on your age, the value of your home, and the current interest rate. And the loan doesn't have to be paid until you sell your home or die. If you take a reverse mortgage loan, you can elect to get your payout in several ways: as a line of credit, a monthly payment, a lump sum, or some combination of the three.

Making More Money

Yes, you are working hard to make ends meet, but sometimes the only way to dig out from under debt is to earn some extra money. According to the Bureau of Labor Statistics, four out of ten Americans are working a second job. Why? Because they need the money to meet their regular living expenses. Moonlighting-holding a second job in addition to a regular one-can take many different forms.

If you decide to moonlight, you may need to let your employer know what you're doing. Most companies don't have written policies on moonlighting. However, it goes without saying that most do not encourage their employees to moonlight. They are concerned that the extra hours one of their employees spends moonlighting will distract him from his regular job. If you decide to moonlight, you are probably better off not disclosing your intent to moonlight in the interest of protecting your regular job. Be sure to check your company's employee handbook if one is available.

How do you start looking for a second job? Looking for a part-time job is much like the steps you went through to find your full-time job. Scan the classified job ads and surf the job boards on the Internet to find leads. Be sure to check out the temporary services as well. When the regular job market is weak, the temporary job market can compensate for the difference. Temporary services cut across all occupations and time slots around the clock.

If you're considering quitting your current job and getting one that pays more, make sure you have a minimum salary figure and fringe benefits in mind that you would accept. You may be able to get the extra money you need from your current job. If it has been a while since you've received a raise, ask for one. If for whatever reason you don't get it; ask your supervisor or manager what you need to do to get a raise. If you get nondescript and meaningless answers, then maybe it is time to review all of your options.

Starting a Home Based Business

If you're considering starting a home based business to make some extra money, there's a catalog called the *Small Business Catalog* you can order free by calling 800-947-7724. Home business guides are featured in the catalog for about $40 per guide, which is a bargain compared to what you'll spend when you actually move into the start-up process. Each guide shows you how to start up a specific home business. You can also order supplemental videos for any of the businesses featured. The catalog offers an easy and inexpensive way to review what the editors consider are the best weekend or full-time home business opportunities. The *Adams Businesses You Can Start Almanac* published by the editors of Adams Media features 500 start-up businesses complete with cost requirements, potential earnings, and the equipment you'll need to get started.

How can you make sure that if you start a home business, it will have a good chance of taking off? Create a dynamic business plan in writing so that you can focus on what you are doing and give your business direction. At a minimum, your business plan should identify your target market with a clear definition of the types of customers who will most likely buy your products or services, where they live, and how you will sell to them. Your plan should also include a twelve-month and three-year cash flow projection that shows all of the sources and dollar amounts for monthly income, expenses, and estimated profits or losses. The following checklist will also help make sure your home business succeeds:

1. Get a good accountant. An accountant can show you how to save thousands of dollars on legitimate tax deductions if you keep good records. Keep your tax records straight by keeping receipts for legitimate business expenses.

2. Open a separate business bank account. It is important from a tax standpoint that you keep business-related expenses and income separate from your personal expenses. Get a business license from your city and state, which will entitle

you to buy products at wholesale from a number of wholesale outlets in your area.

3.   Always have a separate telephone number for your home business. You won't impress any customers who call and get your four-year-old on the phone while they are trying to order something.

4.   You must be able to accept payments from Visa and Master Card. Yes, there is a service fee that you'll have to pay, but you don't want to turn down a sale because you can't accept a customer's card.

Seeking Professional Advice

Do you need debt counseling and support? If you made it this far in the book and you still have no idea what you need to do to get out of debt, consider getting help from a credit counselor. They can put you on a "debt management program" or DMP. If you apply and they accept you as a client (you can be turned down if they don't believe you're serious), your counselor will arrange for you to pay off your debts usually at a lower interest rate. In exchange, you have to agree to stop using your credit cards and applying for additional credit. From this point on, you make one payment (usually monthly). If you need psychological support, you may be able to find a support group in your area. These are people just like you who are trying to get out of debt. Start your search on the Internet at *www.simpleliving.net.* There is also Debtors Anonymous, which is a twelve-step program that's based on the same principles as Alcoholics Anonymous. Reach them at *www.debtors anonymous.org.*

Chapter 9

Protecting Yourself With Insurance

Nobody likes to pay for insurance until they need it

Failing to protect your financial well-being without adequate insurance is like jumping out of an airplane without a parachute. You will eventually hit the ground. The question is how hard do you want to hit it? Your emergency fund plan should include a list of insurance policies you currently have, complete with policy numbers, the amount of coverage, and what exactly is covered. Identify any policies where you believe coverage needs to be increased, decreased, or eliminated. Next, list any additional insurance coverage you may need (e.g., medical insurance) and set a date as to when you'll get it. Review the insurance part of your financial plan at least every six months to keep it current with any changes in your life.

Even though you may be up to your neck in debt and insurance is the last thing on your "must have" list, you still need to consider all of your insurance options. If you don't have any insurance or a sufficient amount of the right insurance, everything you own can be in jeopardy. A single sickness or accident could wipe you out. If you think it could never happen to you, think again! Your insurance plan should be an important part of your overall financial plan. It should cover your financial needs in the event that a disaster adversely affects you financially. If you're married and living off two incomes, you and your spouse need to address the financial ramifications of one of you dying prematurely. Could the surviving spouse sustain his or her lifestyle on a single income? If children are involved, the scenario needs to be expanded to cover their financial needs if one or both of you were to die before they reach adulthood.

Life Insurance

You don't need any life insurance if no one whom you care about will suffer from the financial consequences of your untimely death. If this statement applies to you, then skip the questions on life insurance. Like auto insurance or homeowners insurance, term insurance buys you pure protection at lower cost than whole life insurance. The premiums are usually paid annually at a set term and increase as you age. Its sole function is to provide financial support to your family or people you care about if you die. On the surface, term insurance would seem to be preferable to whole life since it is considerably cheaper. Term policies end in a specified number of years, such as ten or twenty.

If you still need insurance coverage when your term policy runs out, you can always renew it if you're in good health. If you develop health problems like high blood pressure, you may be uninsurable, which is a major disadvantage of term insurance. Term insurance is great if you need a lot of cheap life insurance coverage over a specified number of years while you simultaneously replace the protection it provides by building your investment portfolio. Whole life insurance remains in effect for the rest of your life, regardless of your physical condition.

If you're married and have children, one approach would be to multiply the combined incomes of you and your spouse by the number of years your children will be dependents to get a ballpark minimum coverage figure. For example, let's assume that you and your spouse have a combined annual income of $75,000. You have two children, ages eight and ten, who you have decided will remain dependents until they reach the age of eighteen. The amount of life insurance coverage could be calculated as follows:

Coverage = (Combined Incomes) x (Dependent Years
Remaining / Number of Dependents)
= ($75,000) x (10 + 8) /2
= $75,000 x 9 years
= $675,000

Each spouse would need to purchase a life insurance policy equal to one half of the total amount needed, or $337,500, to be able to cover the lost income if one of them were to die. In this example, it was arbitrarily assumed that each spouse earns the same amount of money, or $37,500 a year, to simplify the illustration.

When you shop for life insurance, contact at least two companies that you can negotiate with at the same time. All of them have different life products to offer at widely varying fees. You can check their ability to pay in the event of a death by the company's rating, which is AAA for the highest rating, BBB for the next best, and so on. You can find insurance company ratings at *www.msure.com*. Select an insurance agent that you are comfortable with and who is willing to present the pros and cons of several different life insurance policies.

Establish a baseline of what you need. In the interest of keeping it simple, get a price for a plain-vanilla term life policy in the amount that you need. It is the cheapest form of life insurance offered. You buy a specified amount of coverage (e.g., $100,000) for a term of years (e.g., twenty years). At the end of the term, the policy expires. It is as simple as that. All insurance companies would prefer to sell you a whole life policy, or a derivative thereof, rather than a cheap term policy because there is more money in it for them. Whole life policies pay off when you die and typically build up a cash value over time.

As you would expect, they cost a lot more than a term policy. Again, compare their cost and added features to what you would pay for a term policy so that you can make an intelligent decision as to what's best for you. If you are heavily in debt, a plain term policy may be all that you can afford at this time.

Car Insurance

The following list covers a description of auto insurance options along with a brief explanation of what's important:

Bodily injury liability. Liability coverage protects you financially if your car injures or kills someone. Because you could be liable for a large sum, you should obtain as much of this coverage as you can afford. Because of your debt situation, you may have to settle for the minimum liability amount that is required by your state.

Collision and comprehensive coverage. Collision coverage pays for damage to your vehicle, no matter who is at fault. Premiums vary with the value of a vehicle and the amount of the deductible. If you are driving an older car, it may not pay to buy collision coverage, unless it would cost you a lot more to replace what you have currently. Comprehensive coverage picks up where collision leaves off. It insures your vehicle against theft, damage from falling objects, earthquakes, floods, or collisions with animals.

Property damage liability. If you are at fault, property damage pays for the damage that your car causes to another person's car, but it also covers any damage your car might do to other property, such as a trailer or a home. Because of your debt situation, you may have to settle for the minimum liability amount that is required by your state.

Medical payments. This pays for medical bills from injuries suffered in an accident. It's a relatively inexpensive form of medical insurance and pays the medical bills for anybody injured in your car regardless of who was at fault.

Uninsured and underinsured motorist coverage. This covers you if you're involved in an accident with an uninsured driver or a driver who is underinsured.

Disability Insurance

Do you need it? Yes, if you are working in a high personal-risk job like construction. Disability insurance pays you a monthly income if you are not able to work because of an illness or an accident. You insure yourself for a specified sum of money, such as $5,000 a month or whatever you need to get by. You may already have disability insurance, so check with your human resources department to find out if you're covered. You can buy individual coverage that can be standalone coverage or a supplement to coverage you already have.

Most major insurance companies offer some form of disability insurance. Many professional and trade associations offer different forms of inexpensive disability insurance. If you don't have disability insurance, see if it is available through an organization that you belong to. Because of your debt situation, you may not be able to afford disability insurance at this time.

Health and Dental Insurance

Explore as many options as you can, and find something that you can afford. You need a health plan that will insure your continued good health. Without health insurance, it will be difficult for you to find a doctor, and you could even be turned away from a hospital emergency room unless it is a life-or-death situation. Health insurance premiums have risen significantly in the past four years alone with no end in sight.

Health maintenance organization (HMO) plans are "managed care" plans in which you are limited as to the doctors you can go to, since the doctors must be in the plan. You may need to pay to see a provider doctor in order to get a script or a referral to a doctor outside of the HMO plan. A preferred provider organization (PPO) plan gives you more flexibility in choosing your doctor and getting tests approved for payment. As a general rule, the more flexibility you have in choosing your doctors, the greater the cost of the plan.

If you have health insurance where you work and you leave your employer, check into the availability of COBRA coverage. COBRA (Consolidated Omnibus Budget Reconciliation Act) was an act passed by Congress in 1986 that allows former employees of a company to keep their company health plan for at least eighteen to thirty-six months after leaving the company. Blue Cross and Blue Shield are mandated to insure all people without regard to most of the criteria commercial insurers normally use. Blue Cross is readily available if you are willing to pay their high premiums. Many trade and professional associations now offer medical insurance policies for their members.

What is the best way to shop for affordable health care insurance? First, eliminate insurers that for any reason make you feel uncomfortable, such as those who refuse to insure you for preexisting conditions. Second, consult a knowledgeable associate and use her judgment to help narrow the field. Find out if health insurance is available from any organizations to which you belong. Many religious, fraternal, and professional organizations provide health insurance for their members at competitive rates. If you have health insurance at work and are looking for ways to reduce the cost, ask your benefits person if there is a less expensive plan you could switch to.

If you are paying for your own insurance, go to *www.ehealthinsurance.com* to see if there is a less expensive plan to switch to. If you join an HMO, make sure you know their rules and whom to call if there is ever a question. If you don't follow their rules, they may not pay your medical bills. With a few smart moves, you can cut your prescription drug bills by 50 percent or more. If your doctor prescribes a brand-name drug, always ask if there is a generic equivalent. Partnership for Prescription Assistance (*www.pparx.com;* 888-477-2669) provides a centralized data bank that makes it easy to learn about over 250 public and private discount drug programs.

Dental insurance comes packaged in three general types of policies: A basic policy will cover routine examinations and cleaning, a maintenance policy extends the basic policy to cover some dental work like fillings, and a comprehensive policy covers major dental work that is specifically identified in the wording of the policy. As you increase the options that a dental policy offers, your premiums increase accordingly. Now, do you need dental insurance? If your teeth are in good condition, then you probably do not need it. If they are not in good condition, then you may need dental insurance. One of the best ways to find out is to get a comprehensive dental exam complete with a list of what dental work needs to be done and the cost to restore to "good" the condition of your teeth. Once you know this, you are in a position to shop for a dental policy that meets your needs.

Homeowners Insurance

Most homes are insured with a homeowner's policy that combines property insurance and personal liability insurance into a single policy. The property portion of the insurance covers your home, its furnishings, and your personal belongings. The personal liability part covers individuals or members of a household against claims from third parties who may have sustained an injury while they were on your property. If your home was destroyed by a fire, you would have to spend a considerable amount of money to replace not only your home but your furnishings as well. One of the best opportunities you have to save money on your homeowner's policy without taking on significant additional risk is in the personal property part of your policy, which carries a deductible. The deductible could range anywhere from $0 to $250, $500, $1,000, or more. The higher the deductible, the less you'll pay.

Don't over insure. If your house is worth $100,000 and you insure it for $200,000 and it gets destroyed by fire, the most you'll get is $100,000. That's the way the insurance system works. Don't underinsure for the same reason. If your house is worth $200,000 and you insure it for $100,000, you'll only get $100,000. Install deadbolts, fire detectors, a fire extinguisher, and a burglar alarm (even a cheap one), and you'll get a discount on your insurance. Ask about "replacement value" insurance that does not depreciate your assets regardless of age.

If my home is in what they call a low to medium area for floods, do I need flood insurance? Yes. Approximately 25 percent of the flood insurance claims come from the flood risk areas (e.g., the Midwest). If you are living in a floodplain area, you need flood insurance. Premiums for flood insurance are expensive, but if you have watched a news broadcast showing homes caught in a major flood, you should have an appreciation for the fact that your home can be completely destroyed by a flood. The Federal Emergency

Management Agency (FEMA) offers a National Flood Insurance Program (NFIP) that is available in communities that adopt and enforce regulations to reduce flood losses.

For more information about NFIP, call their office at 888-379-9531 or visit their website at *www.jema.gov. They* can tell you if your area is covered and what its flood risks are. FEMA's guidelines for assessment of risk are based on an anticipated 100-year flood event. If you live near a major river that has a levee, you would be well advised to include flood insurance in your homeowner's policy. If the levee gives out before a 100-year flood, you will have protected all of your home and its furnishings. Flooding is happening more frequently, particularly in the Midwest, as we saw in 2010.

Credit Insurance

Credit insurance is a waste of money. Credit insurance guarantees a lender's loan in the event of your demise, and the companies that sell credit insurance policies make a lot of money off them. It is one of the most expensive decreasing term insurance policies that you can buy. In most cases, you are not the beneficiary of the policy. The lender is the beneficiary of a policy that you pay for. They are not a good deal.

Watch Your Deductibles

An insurance deductible is what you will pay, out of your pocket, before you collect the balance due to you by your insurance provider. For example, if you have a $100 deductible on your health care plan, then you will be responsible for paying the first $100 before your insurance will begin to pay for the rest of your care. You can use deductibles to your advantage because the higher the deductible, the less the insurance plan will cost you. Also, you can often deduct these from your taxes. This can give you some breathing room when it comes to health care costs. For example, if you get a minimal deductible, such as $100, then you will pay more each month than a plan with, say, a $1,000 deductible.

You can usually get a discount on the cost of insurance when you buy all of your insurance from one company. Purchasing your home, car, and health insurance from one provider can save you hundreds of dollars. It is worth getting several quotes from reputable companies and inquiring about combining all of your insurance under their umbrella. Once you have their quote, compare the quotes and coverage with other reputable companies to find the best rates.

Chapter 10

Putting Everything Together

When you put it together, make sure all the parts fit or it won't work

Congratulations you have made it to the final chapter in the book. You're not done however, because steering clear of debt and building financial independence is a lifelong endeavor. The key to your ongoing success is keeping your head above water and staying ahead of the game. This chapter addresses several important issues that will help you make the right financial decisions and protect what you have built.

Taking on the task of getting yourself out of debt is going to present you with some tough challenges, as have been addressed throughout this book. If you are serious about making it happen, then you need to establish a goal that comes from your heart - one that will give you the drive to make it happen. How about setting a goal of becoming financially independent? That sounds good, but what does that mean? Becoming financially independent means you have secured sources of income that will support a lifestyle that's acceptable to you for the rest of your life without having to rely on borrowed money.

The Key to Staying Out of Debt

As you begin to eliminate your debt, your wealth will grow. You'll be able to retire even more of your debt as you move forward and for the first time, begin to feel in control of your money. But, no matter how carefully you plan or how committed you are to your goals, stuff can happen. You can lose a job, suffer an illness, or be thrown off-track in any number of ways that can disrupt your ability to reach some of your goals. If that happens, be prepared to rethink your goals and implement a new plan. That's all part of the game, and if you get discouraged, just remembers that winners are the ones who never give up.

This book started out by showing you multiple ways to save money. Why? Because you should have some extra money that you could invest in the wide variety of investment vehicles covered throughout the book. Making, saving, and investing money the smart way takes discipline, time, and patience. If you're not willing to do that, you'll never achieve financial independence. The irony is that it really doesn't take much effort to become financially secure if you are willing to practice self-discipline now, for future peace of mind and prosperity.

If you start with a budget, a solid set of financial goals, and work out from there, you will become financially independent. As you begin to climb out of debt, invest your money wisely. Set up and religiously deposit money into a savings account. Make sure that you have an emergency fund so that you can pay for emergency expenses instead of charging them on credit cards. Develop a basic understanding of investment options like stocks, mutual funds, bonds, and money market funds. As you begin to save money, invest it in securities that fit with where you want to go financially.

Use debit cards instead of credit cards. Debit cards draw money from your checking account to pay for a purchase. They don't allow you to overspend the way credit cards do. Place your credit cards in a safe, out-of-the-way place and use them only for legitimate financial emergencies. Buy and keep a home and drive a car that's paid for.

Become Financially Independent

Financial independence is a goal that we all would like to achieve at some stage of our lives (i.e., retirement). It's as much a state of mind as it is money. Lots of us spend all kinds of time thinking and talking about how we are going to achieve it, but few of us are willing to actually take any action to make it happen. There are some excellent resources that are offered at a minimal cost or free to anyone who is interested. A great website that offers a variety of articles pertaining to financial freedom is *www.money.cnn.com*. It may also be worthwhile to consider a subscription to a monthly magazine such as *Kiplinger's Personal Finance Magazine* or *Money*.

Magazines can be a helpful reminder to keep you on your financial track when you receive the magazine every month through your mail. Of course, books on this topic are plentiful and can be checked out at your local library for free or ordered used and at a discounted price through *www.amazon.com.A* couple of suggested books are *The 9 Steps to Financial Freedom* by Suze Orman or *The Six-Day Financial Makeover* by Robert Pagliarini. Here's a summary of the steps they all advocate:

Set financial goals. To be meaningful, a goal must be very specific, with a designated completion date assigned to it. Start with small, relatively simple financial goals such as opening a savings account this week. As you become more comfortable in the goal-setting process, move up to intermediate goals like making regular monthly deposits into your IRA.

Avoid unnecessary debt. If, for example, you want to take a cruise to Alaska but you don't have the money, wait until you do. If you don't have the money, don't use credit cards to get it. Buy a home and invest wisely. It is one of the best tax shelters you can get. Pay off your home mortgage faster by sending your payment coupons in early along with an extra payment. Make sure you state to the lender that payment goes toward the principal.

Drive a car that's paid for. There is nothing better than a car that's paid for. Don't rush out to trade it in just because the loan is paid off. If Old Faithful is still running, keep it and save the money.

Save and invest your money. You need a savings plan that is flexible but firm, and, most important, is something you can stick to. Your first challenge will be to get control over your spending habits and establish a monthly budget for everything you buy. If you can start saving on even the little things, it will add up to big dollars over a relatively short period of time.

Start a Financial Plan

A financial plan consolidates into a single plan everything that you have learned and want to do up to this point. All of the notes that you've taken on spending less, consolidating debt, reducing what you're spending on insurance and the wealth of other debt-related topics that we've covered can be assembled into a binder or file folder so that the material is at your fingertips when you need it.

You need a financial plan because it is your starting point for getting out of debt. In all probability, you did not get into debt overnight. It took time and happened because of a number of financial decisions that you made. Unfortunately, your debt won't just go away with a wish and a prayer. It's going to take planning and hard work to make that happen.

What are the essential components of a financial plan? Include a list of specific financial objectives in the front of your plan. For example, it might include a college education for one of your kids, a down payment on a home, or an emergency savings plan. Place dividers in your planning binder for the following sections:

Income Plan: Here is where you show your monthly take home pay and any sources of additional income that you might have.

Spending Plan: This section includes your monthly budget supplemented with a written spending plan that shows how you will meet specific expense categories and control your expenses.

Saving Plan: What you plan to save each month is shown in your saving plan. Show where the money will come from and how it will be deposited into your savings account.

Security Plan: Identify each insurance policy that you have, what is covered, and when the premium payments are due. Include any notes you may have to reduce or increase your insurance premiums.

Tax Plan: Identify the steps that you are planning to take to reduce taxes. Outline the tax deductions that you intend to take and what rate you're in.

Retirement Plan: Contributions that you are making into retirement accounts like IRAs are identified in this section, which will complete your investment plan.

After you've put your financial plan together, you are ready for a "critical evaluation" of your plan. If you haven't documented your plan in writing, complete with spreadsheets that project income and expenses throughout your life, then you don't have a plan that's worth considering. When you are confident that you have a solid plan, have it reviewed by a professional, such as a CPA, accountant, or certified financial planner. Of course, this review will cost you money up-front. However, think about it as a small price to pay to ensure that your plan is solid and tight. It's okay to include contingency plans in your master plan if certain assumptions that you have made don't work out. In fact, if you don't have lots of contingencies built into your plan, you probably don't have a solid plan.

Invest Wisely

You want your hard-earned money to continue to grow and prosper. To do that, you need to begin building an investment portfolio that encompasses your goals and time horizon. Your ultimate goal may be to become financially independent. How soon you want to make that happen and in what standard of living style can significantly affect your decisions on how you invest your money. How you choose to diversify (e.g., stocks, bonds, mutual funds) depends on your rate-of-return goals, how much risk you can tolerate, and how long you can invest your money.

Rate of return (ROR) is a measure of the money an investor makes when he invests in something like a stock or an antique clock. It is typically reflected as an annualized percentage increase of what you sold an investment for over what you paid for it. For example, if you purchased a share of stock for $100 and sold it one year later for

111

$110, you would have enjoyed a 10 percent ROR profit ($110/$100 = 1.10). If you purchased a share of stock for $110 and sold it one year later for $100, you would have a 9 percent ROR loss ($100/$110 = .90). A positive ROR is an investor's reward for the risk he has taken to make an investment. High-risk investments demand higher rates of return. At a minimum, you should expect an ROR that exceeds 5 percent because you can easily get that through a "no risk" money market fund. Your rate of return depends on how well the portfolio of securities is doing at any one time.

Manage Your Retirement Plans

As you begin to eliminate each component of your debt load, use the debt-free money to begin to max out your retirement accounts (IRAs, 401(k) plans, etc.). If you are fifty or older, you can start taking advantage of what is called catch-up contributions, which allow you to contribute an extra $5,000 to your 401(k) and an extra $1,000 to a Roth IRA. That's a total of $20,000 through your employee 401(k) contribution of $15,000 and an additional $5,000 for your catch -up contribution. You can also have up to $5,000 for a Roth IRA by adding $4,000 from your

If you don't have an IRA, you need ONE. IRAs, both traditional and Roth, are one of the few investment options left that allow your earnings to grow, tax-free, until you elect to withdraw some or all of the funds that are in your account. Generally, you should first contribute to employer-sponsored plans such as a 401(k) plan to enjoy their matching contributions before you consider opening an IRA account. Before you open an IRA account, make sure you know the rules. As a general rule, don't even think about tapping the money in your IRA until you are fifty-nine and a half or older. There's a 10 percent early withdrawal penalty and you'll pay income tax on anything you take out of the account. If you become totally disabled or need the money to pay for medical expenses, the IRS waives the early withdrawal penalties. Check the regulations first before you make any withdrawals. There are literally thousands of ways to set up an IRA account (see website in the Appendix). If you want to invest IRA funds in CDs, then go to a bank. If you want to invest in mutual funds or stocks, contact a mutual fund company directly or see a stockbroker.

Roth IRAs are different from traditional IRAs. The major differences between a Roth IRA and a traditional IRA are the way in which they are funded and in the rules governing withdrawing funds from them. Roth IRAs are funded with your income dollars after taxes have been withdrawn. Traditional IRAs are funded with your income dollars before taxes have been withdrawn. Consequently, you are not taxed on any funds that you withdraw from a Roth IRA and you can withdraw funds from a Roth IRA at any time, regardless of your age, without incurring a penalty. With a traditional IRA, you're taxed on withdrawals. This is not necessarily a bad thing, since your tax rate may be lower when you retire. You must start withdrawals from a traditional IRA by age seventy and a half.

Self-directed IRAs are set up so that you choose and manage the investments in your account yourself. Most brokers and mutual funds offer them. They may have a small annual fee (usually $50 or less per year) that they charge for this service. Most self-directed IRAs offer a wide variety of investment options for you to consider. To open an IRA account, contact your financial institution or mutual fund representative. If you want to learn more about self-directed IRAs, go to *www.selfdirectedira.org*.

Invest in Funds

Mutual funds have become an extremely popular way to invest for people who don't have the time to conduct their own investment analysis. Today, there are thousands of funds to choose from with a vast range of investment and diversification options, from ultraconservative bond funds to aggressive stock funds that specialize in fast-growth companies. When you invest in a mutual fund, you're buying shares in a portfolio of securities managed by a professional investment firm. Some funds specialize in only one type of security or industry, while others invest in a variety of securities to minimize risk. And not all funds invest in stocks. Many specialize in the bond market and commodities, and the international markets as well.

There are over a thousand mutual funds to choose from, so finding the one that is right for you can be a tedious task. How can you find the better funds? There are a number of books out there that specialize in investing in funds. For example, *Morningstar Guide to Mutual Funds: Five-Star Strategies for Success* by Christine Benz gives you a quick roundup of investment tips. Use research tools. *Barron's* magazine and the *Wall Street Journal* publish fund performance data. Don't ignore the ads in newspapers and financial magazines. Fund companies like to advertise their better-performing funds. To start you off on the Internet, go to *uruno.morningstar.com, www.kiplinger.com,* and *www.investools.com* are three sites that can help you select funds that meet your parameters. The key advantages of mutual funds are summarized as follows:

Diversification. When you invest in a fund, your money is riding on a large number of securities instead of just a few, which lessens the risk.

Low cost management. Professional management fees typically run around 1 percent of your investment annually. You can sell your mutual funds any time, just like a stock.

Flexibility. If you've invested in one of the funds offered by a company like Fidelity Investments that offers investors a family of funds, you can switch between the funds in the family as market conditions or your investment objectives change, at no additional cost.

Typically, you can buy or sell funds directly through brokerage companies like Schwab's OneSource, Vanguard's Fund Access, and Fidelity's Funds Network.

Where to Save

There are several investments for you to consider that are safe places to hold your money. And they all offer interest rates that are substantially better than what you'll get in traditional savings accounts. Insured money market funds are pools of money that are invested in short-term debts issued by the government, the nation's most creditworthy companies, and banks. Certificates of deposits are one of the safest investments you can make since they are insured for up to $100,000. You can buy them from banks and credit unions. The price of most CDs start at $500 and go up from there. They are designed to mature at different lengths of time and offer rates that fluctuate daily. Shop around for the best rates in your area or check Bank Rate Monitor's website *(www.bankrate.com)* for current rates. U.S. Savings Bonds can be purchased for as little as $25 each. If you use them for college expenses, the interest they earn is tax free. Some employers offer them through payroll deduction plans, or you can purchase them through savings and loan associations.

Take Care of Your Estate

Everybody needs a will, whether you are single or married, young or old, healthy or sick. By organizing your estate to your best advantage, you can ensure that your hard -earned money stays in the family or goes to the people and organizations of your choice. A will not only instructs your survivors about how to distribute your property; it also enables you to nominate a guardian to care for your children should they become orphaned. You designate someone whom you trust to act as your estate's executor (e.g., your spouse). This person will be responsible for paying off your creditors and taxes, and ultimately splitting your estate among your heirs in accordance with the wishes you document in your will.

An estate plan arranges the distribution of assets in your estate when you die or if you become incapacitated. It can be used to make your wishes known in regard to your finances and personal care. Most estate planning begins with a will, which specifies who gets your property when you die. A living will is a supplemental document to a will. It allows you to spell out the medical treatment you want under specific circumstances. For example, you can specify whether you want life-support equipment under certain medical conditions so that your family members don't have to make the difficult decision on your behalf. Your estate plan is the final component of your financial plan. It's your assurance that everything you have worked for all your life will be distributed to your loved ones, according to your wishes.

When you create your will, consider using an estate-planning attorney to help draft the document. You can draft one from do-it-yourself personal computer software, but any savings you may incur over attorney fees are hardly worth the risk of a mistake or oversight on your part. If you prefer to write your own will, you should do so only if your will is not complicated. Quicken offers a software product called Will Maker that is available at computer stores and online (*www.nolo.com*).

Social Security and Medicare

As a general rule, social security will cover about 25 percent of your preretirement income (less if you're rich, more if you're poor). Social security uses a formula to calculate what is called your Average Indexed Monthly Earnings (AIME) at retirement. Currently, your payment is based on 90 percent of the first $592 of your monthly income, 32 percent of the next $2,975, and then 15 percent of the amount over $3,567.The maximum monthly benefit you can receive at age sixty-five is $1,874 per month. Your social security income is tax-free unless you are married and your annual earnings are more than $32,000 or single with earnings exceeding $25,000, including half of your social security. A maximum of 85 percent will be taxable if your adjusted annual income on a joint return reaches $44,000 ($35,000 for singles).

Every year, call the Social Security Administration (800-772-1213) and ask them to send you form SSA -7004 for your personal earnings and benefits estimate. Start checking their records against your annual VV-2 forms to make sure they recorded every dollar you paid into social security. Yes, when all of the "baby boomers" retire, the social security system will be financially strained and the federal government has been borrowing heavily from the fund to finance the national debt. However, the government is determined to keep the program.

116

Unfortunately, you can expect your health costs to increase as you get older. To cover this issue, make sure you absolutely know what is and is not covered by Medicare and any private insurance you may have. Determine what your part is of any co-pay requirement. Typically, your insurer pays 80 percent and you pay 20 percent. Do not forget to include prescription drug costs in your estimates.

Seek Advice

Many resources are available to help you prepare for your financial future, like retirement. Some sources are listed here for your convenience. If you enjoy reading books, try Barnes & Noble's website *(www.barnesandnoble.com)* or Amazon's website *(www.amazon.com)* and browse through their retirement book sections. If you prefer researching online, check out Charles Schwab's site, which will help you develop a retirement plan with their online calculators, tools, and advice. Go to their home page at *www.schwab.com* and click on Advice & Retirement at the top of the menu. This section should help you get started. If you have a question or need advice on your financial plan, you may want to consult one of the following professionals:

Accountant for tax advice, tax strategies and the preparation of tax returns.

Insurance agent for insurance coverage issues and policy information.

Stockbroker or mutual fund agent for investing in stocks and bonds. They can also provide you with information pertaining to money market funds.

Banker for information on savings and certificate of deposit accounts.

Financial planner for general advice on finances including the spending, saving, insurance, and investment sections of your financial plan.

A good financial planner is a one-stop money consultant. They in theory know a little something about everything in the financial planning field. They can help you uncover the problems that caused your past debt, help you formulate new financial goals, and develop an implementation plan. They can also help you merge your savings into an investment plan. A majority of planners make their living selling insurance policies, tax-deferred annuities, mutual funds, stocks, and their consultation time. Many financial planners do tax returns.

How do you find a good financial planner? You can obtain a directory of the financial planners who are in your area by contacting The National Association of Personal Financial Advisors (800-555-6659 or *www.napfa.org)*, The American Institute of Certified Public Accountants Personal Financial Division (800-862-4272 or *http://pfP.aicpa.org/resources)*, or The Financial Planning Association (800-282-7526 or *www.fPanet.org)*.

When you begin to make your initial screening calls for a planner, let them know as specifically as you can why you're seeking help and ask them what services they offer. Listen carefully to their answers to help you determine if they have the expertise you need. Ask them for the names of at least three clients whom you can contact who have been with them for at least two years, and make sure you contact these clients to determine their level of satisfaction. Ask the planner how they are paid. They should be willing to disclose all of their compensation requirements in detail. If they won't do this, scratch them off your list and proceed to your next candidate.

In conclusion, it is sincerely hoped that all of the get-out-of debt ideas covered in this book will help you keep more of what you have today and achieve the financial success tomorrow that you deserve. We want to wish you the very best in your efforts toward achieving financial independence.

Appendix A

Glossary of Terms

401(k) plan is a broad label for a variety of employer-sponsored retirement savings incentive programs.

403(b) plan is a retirement plan available to employees of public schools, nonprofit organizations, or the clergy. It is identical to the 401(k), except that employers need not contribute, and they aren't subject to 401(k)'s stringent Employee Retirement Income Security Act (ERISA).

457 deferred-compensation plan sometimes called a deferred-camp plan, this retirement plan defers an employee's pay by the amount contributed, a characteristic shared by 401(k) and SIMPLE plans.

Account aggregator is an online platform that presents data from multiple accounts in a single interface that stores log-in information and simplifies web access to personal financial information.

Accrual method is an accounting method often used by businesses with inventory; with this method, you report income and deduct expenses when the work's done (you've done all the things you have to do to get paid and all the expenses have been incurred).

Active management is an investment management style that presumes that investments guided by a fund manager and informed by industry and economic insight should perform better than other similar investments.

Adjusted gross income (AGI) is the amount of income calculated by adding work income and other income such as investment interest and dividends or alimony. It excludes such things as alimony paid and the cost of health insurance paid by the self-employed.

Administrative fees are the fees that cover the cost of running the plan itself, including expenses such as the cost of preparing annual reports, running required discrimination tests, and supporting the website and customer service department.

Advertising is a means of informing the public about your product or service.

After-tax contributions are contributions to an IRA that is not deductible from a filer's tax obligation.

Age Discrimination in Employment Act was passed in 1967 and prohibits any employer from refusing to hire, discharge, or discriminate in any way based on a person's age.

Alternative minimum tax was created to close loopholes that enabled some super-rich taxpayers to pay unfairly low or even no taxes by resorting to legal tax shelters. Unfortunately, the tax lacks indexes to inflation, making more middle-class families vulnerable to assessment.

Angels are private investors willing to lend money or equity capital in much the same way as venture capitalists, but on a much smaller scale.

Annual expense ratio is the percentage of plan assets that are paid to cover operating, management, and marketing costs.

Annuity is a financial contract. You buy an annuity with the guarantee that the company-usually an insurance company-will provide a series of regular, fixed payments in exchange. Annuities come in a variety of forms.

Asset allocation is an investment recipe for all an individual's accounts, dictating the percentage of a portfolio invested in stocks, bonds, or cash.

Assisted living is a kind of housing that provides a modest amount of assistance, including bathing, dressing, and cooking meals.

Baby boomers are people born in a flourish of family-boosting activity that followed World War II and continued into the 1960s.

Balance sheet is a listing of assets, liabilities, and an owner's investment in a business as of a fixed date, such as the end of a quarter or year.

Basis is the amount you paid for property (called cost basis) or other amount treated as your investment in property. Adjusted basis is basis increased by additions or improvements and decreased by depreciation.

Benchmark is a standard used to compare performance, such as the Standard and Poor's 500 Index.

Blog is a web log that can be a marketing tool to express your political gripes, position you as an expert, and draw interest to your website.

Board and care is a type of assisted living that generally offers group meals and other activities for residents who want to spend time with friends and neighbors.

Bonds are a form of loan. In buying a bond, you're effectively entering into a contract with the issuer of that bond to pay whatever money you invested, plus interest. Bonds come in a variety of forms.

Book value is the real value of a company. It's calculated by totaling all assets and subtracting debt and liabilities.

Broadband service is a technology that allows the Internet connection to your computer to run faster and better.

Brochure ware is a website that functions like a written brochure, listing your product or services, rates, and contact information.

Business opportunity is a non-franchise arrangement in which you buy a concept for a product or service.

Business plan is a written report describing what a business is all about and where the business is heading in the future.

C Corporation is organized under state law and taxed as a separate person, but treated as a regular corporation.

Call provision are bonds that are paid off prior to their prearranged maturity.

Capital gain tax rate is the percentage of investing profits that must be paid in taxes, calculated as a proportion of the profit or capital gain of an investment.

Career average plans are similar to final pay programs, but based on the average of all the years you work for a company. You may get a percentage of your salary for every year you were in the plan. In other cases, you may get an average for all years you were in the plan.

Cash flow cycle time is the time over which inventory is ordered, paid for, sold, and money is received.

Cash method is an accounting method often used by service businesses. With this method, you record income when your client pays you and deduct expenses as they come up.

Cash value life insurance is a form of life insurance that builds accompanying cash value. These come in several different forms.

Catastrophic coverage is health insurance with exceedingly high deductibles.

Certificates of Deposits (CDs) are a form of promissory note where the lender effectively promises to pay you a certain interest rate if you let them hold your money for a specified amount of time.

COBRA (Consolidated Omnibus Budget Reconciliation Act) requires companies with 20 or more employees to allow you to stay on your health plan for an additional 18 months after you leave your job.

Cohousing is a semi-communal living arrangement where separate living units are arranged around a "common house."

Compounding is the effect of money earning interest which, in turn, results in a larger sum that earns even more.

Congregate housing is a variant of assisted living, offering both a level of assisted care as well as private living space.

Continuing care retirement communities involves several types of housing and living arrangements, including independent living facilities, assisted living, and nursing homes. Retirees can remain in the same retirement community, with the option to change the level of care they receive as their individual needs mandate it.

Conventional IRA was the first Individual Retirement Account introduced and defers any tax impact until you begin to withdraw money from the account.

Custodian is the institution that holds your IRA. It can be a bank, brokerage house, or similar place.

Certificate of deposit is a bank's promissory note to repay the amount deposited, with interest, at a future date, typically one month to five years away.

Chat rooms are locations on the Internet in which people interact with each other on a particular topic or area of mutual interest.

Cliff vesting is a vesting schedule in which none of an employer's contribution becomes an asset of the employee until the employee reaches a specified work anniversary. At the anniversary date, the employer's full contribution belongs to the employee.

Closely held corporation is a privately owned corporation whose stock is not traded on any public exchange.

Collection agency is a business that performs collection services, including sending reminders to late payers and suing delinquents on your behalf.

Commercial loan is money borrowed from a bank or other financial institution that specializes in business lending.

Compound interest is an investment principal in which interest is paid not only on the principal saved but also on the accumulated interest from prior periods that has not been withdrawn.

Constructive receipt is the date when income is treated as having been received by cash-basis businesses because it's under their control, even if they don't actually have the cash in hand (a check is income when received even though you haven't deposited or cashed it yet).

Contribution is an amount of cash or other assets deposited in a retirement account.

Cost of goods sold is the cost of inventory items such as materials, labor, and packaging.

Debt is borrowed money for financing a business. The borrower is called the debtor; the lender is called the creditor.

Deductible for insurance purposes is the amount of damage or liability that the insurance company won't cover. For taxes, it's the amount of expenses you can subtract against income.

Deep discount broker is an investment house that sells stocks and funds very inexpensively.

Defined benefit program is a pension payout based on your salary and number of years of service.

Defined contribution program is a program in which money is automatically deducted from your salary before you take possession of it. From there, the money is put into an investment vehicle of your choosing, including mutual funds, company stock, and other options.

Depreciation is a deduction of a portion of the cost of a car or other equipment you own over the life of the equipment (the life is set by the IRS) to reflect its true value.

Direct rollover is a process that directly transfers assets from one retirement plan into another.

Disability insurance provides income if you become disabled or temporarily unable to earn a living.

Discount brokers charge less than full-service brokers to execute trades.

Dividends are payments to shareholders authorized by a company's board of directors. They can be in cash or additional shares of the company's stock.

Dollar cost averaging is a savings strategy involving investing the same dollar amount at fixed intervals. If share prices increase, fewer shares are bought or if they decrease, more shares are bought at the different intervals.

Domain name is the address n the Internet where people can find your website.

Dow Jones Industrials is a stock index made up of 30 of the largest publicly held companies traded on the New York Stock Exchange.

Dying intestate is the legal term that refers to lack of a will or trust that provides instructions after someone dies.

ECHO is an acronym for Elder Cottage Housing Opportunities. This is usually a separate, small manufactured home that is added onto the side or backyard of an existing home.

Employee stock ownership plan (ESOP) is a program that allows employees to buy company stock, often with little or no commission.

Employer identification number is the number assigned to a business owner by the IRS after you file IRS Form SS-4. This is used for identification purposes on tax returns, bank accounts, and retirement plans.

Endorsement is a correction or change to an existing insurance policy.

Entrepreneur is someone who organizes and directs a start-up business, assuming the risk in the hope of making a profit.

Equity is the value of your home after subtracting the mortgage balance.

Equity financing a business happens when you bring investors in as part owners of the business.

Escrow is an arrangement in which a third party holds funds; when certain conditions are met, the funds are paid out.

Exchange traded funds (ETFs) are pooled investment accounts that resemble mutual funds in that they hold a basket of many individual investments but are traded directly on the stock exchanges by investors buying and selling their shares like stocks.

Expense ratio takes in all expenses incurred by a fund's operations and expresses them in terms of percentages.

Face value is the principal; the amount of money you invested when you bought a bond. It's also known as par value.

Fair market value is what a willing buyer and willing seller would pay, if neither is being forced to buy or sell and each understands all the facts and circumstances of the deal.

Fee for service is a form of health insurance that lets you choose any doctor or health care provider you like. Generally, the coverage pays 80 percent of any costs you accumulate.
You are obligated to pick up the remaining 20 percent.

Fee-only financial planner is a financial advisor who charges only for his advice, based on the consultation duration or project scope, and who doesn't sell investment products for commission in order to avoid conflict of interest in investment choice recommendations.

FICA (Federal Insurance Contributions Act) is the Social Security and Medicare taxes on wages paid by both the employer and the employee.

Final pay plan is a pension that can offer the biggest payout, as they average your salary over the last several years you're employed at a company.

Financial statement is information about income, expenses, sales figures, and other number-oriented items such as a cash flow statement, balance sheet, or profit and loss statement.

Fixed annuity is a tax deferred financial instrument marketed by insurance companies and brokerage firms that pays a fixed rate of interest that readjusts annually. Fixed Annuities are similar to CDs in that they pay a fixed rate of interest that readjusts on a yearly basis. Annuities are sold by life insurance companies and some brokerage firms.

Flat benefit plan is one of the most simple and straightforward pension payout. You receive a set monthly amount based on how long you worked for a company.

Flexible spending account is a program that allows you to set aside money from your salary tax-free. These funds can then be used to help pay for medical expenses that are not covered by your employer's health plan.

Franchise is a business arrangement that gives you the right to sell a product or service in a particular area. The company selling the concept is the franchisor; you are the franchisee. The right to a large territory is called a master franchise.

Fulfillment company is a business that takes and processes orders for you, including acceptance of payment by credit card. Generally, a fulfillment company charges a flat fee.

Full retirement age is the age at which you can receive your full retirement benefit from Social Security.

Fund family is several different mutual funds that a company maintains and offers to clients. The funds are usually set up for different financial objectives.

Fundamental analysis is a stock analysis involving examination of a company's operating statistics and numbers.

FUTA (Federal Unemployment Tax Act) is the Federal unemployment insurance tax paid by an employer on an employee's wages.

Goodwill is a favorable reputation of a business, which is considered an intangible asset.

Graded vesting is a vesting schedule in which an employer's contribution vests gradually over time, in stages or grades.

Grants are money from government sources or private foundations to start or run a business that matches the goals of the grant maker; grant money doesn't have to be repaid. .

Gross income is income before deductions. For purposes of the home office deduction, gross income means money from business minus expenses that don't relate to the use of the home such as office supplies or the salary of an employee.

Guaranteed investment contracts (GICs) is a contract involving a guaranteed rate of return.

Hobby loss rules are the tax rules that prevent an individual from deducting business expenses that are greater than business income where there's no reasonable expectation of making a profit from the business.

Home equity line of credit is a loan secured by the amount of equity you have in your home.

Home-office deduction is the total of deductions from the business use of a home office, including depreciation on the office or a portion of rent, as well as the portion of utilities and insurance related to the home office.

HTML (Hypertext Markup Language) is the programming language used on computers to create websites.

Independent contractor is a person who contracts to provide work according to his own methods. This person isn't under the control of the person or business for which the work is being performed (not an employee).

Income tax rate is the percentage of one's income that must be paid to local, state, or federal government.

Individual retirement accounts (IRA) are planned accounts that carry a tax advantage intended to encourage savings.

Individual 401(k) is a retirement savings program best suited for someone who works on their own and has no plans to bring on any employees in the future.

Inflation is the effect of rising prices on the value of money to buy goods and services.

Irrevocable trust is a trust that can't be changed in any way during the grantor's lifetime.

Internet is a worldwide collection of computer networks that you can access with a computer, modem, telephone line, and an online service provider or Internet service provider.

Invoice is an itemized list of products you've sold to someone, stating the quantity, price, and terms of sale; a bill for services rendered.

IRA basis is the amount contributed to an IRA that isn't eligible for tax deduction.

IRA trustee fees are costs paid by the investor that can include sales commissions, management fees, and marketing fee.

Joint and several liabilities is a legal rule that makes two or more parties fully responsible for damages, debt repayment, and other legal obligations.

Keogh plan is a tax-deferred retirement plan that lets small business owners and the self-employed save money for retirement.

Lifestyle funds are investment pools that resemble target-date funds in that they are a mix of mutual funds in an asset allocation that the mutual fund company chooses but that cater to risk tolerances.

Limited liability company is a type of business organization formed under state law that gives owners protection from personal liability but treats them as a partnership for tax purposes.

Limited partnership is a partnership in which one or more partners has limited personal liability and can't participate in the day-to-day operations of the business.

Limit orders is a stock purchase system that lets you establish prices at which you wish to buy or sell.

Living will also known as an advanced medical directive, this is a document that outlines your decisions about any sort of life-sustaining treatment.

Long-term care insurance is insurance you buy to pay for nursing home care and other sorts of long-term, comprehensive care.

Managed care also known as health maintenance organizations, is less expensive than fee for service. However, you have a limited choice of health care providers.

Medicaid is the federal program designed to pay for health care for the poor.

Medicare is the federal medical care program for persons age 65 and up. It is subdivided into four parts, offering different forms of coverage.

Medigap insurance is supplemental insurance to cover any gaps in Medicare coverage.

Marginal tax rate is the rate on the highest bracket a taxpayer's income reached.

Marketing is how people advertise, publicize, or otherwise inform each other of their product or service with the goal of exchanging products or services with each other.

Matching contribution is the employer plan-match option under which an employer promises to match a certain percentage of each employee's contribution up to a specific percentage of their pay.

Medical IRA known as a health savings account is an individual retirement account in which account holders can deposit pretax money to pay for medical expenses.

Modified adjusted gross income known as modified AGI, is the adjusted gross income from an IRA withdrawal by someone age

591/2 or older, disabled or deceased, using the withdrawals to pay for college or other qualified higher education expenses, or using withdrawals toward a first-time home purchase.

Money market deposit account is an investment account that often pays lower interest than a CD, but whose assets are accessible anytime without waiting for a future maturity date.

Money market fund is an investment account whose the cash in the account is accessible at anytime.

Monte Carlo calculator is a calculator that generates a measure of the probability that a given investment outcome scenario will result in a financially comfortable retirement based on expected assets, probable lifetime, and economic conditions.

Mutual funds are a combination of individual investments such as stocks, bonds, and cash bundled together into one product.

Net operating losses are business expenses in excess of business income; business losses that can be carried back 2 years and forward 20 years; also called NOLs.

Net unrealized appreciation is the difference in value between the average cost that you paid for stock and its current market value.

Network marketing is direct sales to consumers with distributors getting money from both direct sales and a percentage of the direct sales of other distributors they bring into the network.

Networking is word-of-mouth marketing in which contacts are made to try to drum up business.

Nonretirement accounts are bank or mutual fund accounts that are not held inside IRAs and on which taxes must be paid as accrued.

Overhead is the cost of monthly expenses, including electricity, telephone, insurance, and salaries of employees.

Partnership occurs when two or more people working together in a business with the intention of making a profit.

Passive management is an investment management style that seeks to match the market's performance.

Personal service corporation is subject to special tax rules; corporation engaged in the fields of health, law, accounting, engineering, architecture, actuarial science, performing arts, or consulting that meets certain ownership and service tests.

Plan provider is the company hired by an employer to administer their retirement plan, who often acting as the plan's trustee as well.
Points represent an up-front interest payment to a lender. One point is equivalent to 1 percent of the amount borrowed.

Power of attorney allows someone to make decisions when you're incapable of doing so yourself. Examples include medical and financial power of attorney.

Pretax contribution to a tax deferred retirement amount that a filer is permitted to deduct from their tax obligation.

Price-earnings ratio (PIE) is a popular stock ratio that illustrates how much an investor would be willing to spend in return for $1 in company earnings.

Price/book ratio (PIB) is a ratio that compares a stock's price to what a company is worth.

Price/sales ratio (P/S) is ratio that is calculated by dividing a current stock price by a company's earnings per share.

Primary insurance amount (PIA) is all your Social Security cash benefits, including your monthly benefit as well as benefits for dependents and survivors.

Probate is the legal process that the state must go through should you die with property still in your name.

Prime rate is the interest rate banks charge their preferred customers.

Profit sharing contribution is an employer contribution to their employees' retirement account that is made based on the profits of the company.

Promotion is the act of stimulating an immediate sale with special offers, such as discount coupons.

Publicly held corporation issues stock that is traded on a public exchange such as the New York Stock Exchange.

QUADRO is a divorce-specific transfer between two people's accounts requiring a court order.

Qualified is a term that means a pension program has to adhere to certain governmental guidelines for tax purposes.

Real estate investment trusts (REITs) are funds that invest in property, including shopping centers, apartment buildings, and similar commercial operations.

Rebalancing are adjustments to an asset allocation that correct for different assets having performed differently over time, eventually comprising different portfolio percentages than intended.

Reverse mortgage is a mortgage that lets you tap the accumulated equity in your home. In doing so, your loan balance increases rather than going down.

Revocable trust is a trust that may be changed or eliminated completely.

Rider is an additional clause to an existing contract or insurance policy to cover a special item or event (usually an upgrade to a policy); sometimes referred to as an endorsement.

Risk tolerance is the amount of uncertainty and volatility with which an investor feels comfortable.

Roth 401(k) is an employer-sponsored retirement account in which tax liability accrues upon contribution but whose account earnings and withdrawals are tax-free.

Roth 403(b) is an employer-sponsored retirement account offered to employees of public schools, nonprofit organizations, and the clergy in which tax liability accrues upon contribution but whose account earnings and withdrawals are tax-free.

Roth IRA is a form of individual retirement account in which taxes do not accrue on withdrawn funds, whether earnings or basis.

S Corporation also called a Subchapter S Corporation is organized under state law that elects to have business income taxed to its shareholders.

Safe-harbor 401(k) is an employee-sponsored plan that reduces an employer's effort and cost in running the plan's nondiscrimination tests.

SBA (Small Business Administration) is a federal agency that sponsors loan programs and other assistance to small businesses.

SBICs (Small Business Investment Companies) are privately managed firms licensed by the SBA to make loans to small businesses.

Search engines are websites that enable you to find other pages on the web, just like a library card catalog helps you find books on shelves.

Self-employment tax is Social Security and Medicare taxes paid by self-employed individuals, such as sole proprietors, on their net earnings from the business.

Self-insured is having sufficient assets to make life insurance unnecessary.

SEP plan known as the Simplified Employee Pension plan is a retirement option popular with people who are self-employed and who don't have employees in which 100 percent of the contributions come from the employer.

Shareholders are the owners of a corporation (also called stockholders) whose ownership interest is in the form of stock certificates.

Shares outstanding are the total number of shares owned by an investor.

SIMPLE 401(k) plan is a plan that combines the features of SIMPLE IRAs and regular 401(k) plans, including contribution limits and employer match rules of SIMPLE plans.

SIMPLE IRA is an acronym for Savings Incentive Match Plan. This type of IRA is particularly suited to someone whose self-employment income is relatively modest-$30,000 annually or less.

SIMPLE Plan also known as the Savings Incentive Match Plan for Employees is a common option in companies with 30 or fewer employees but available to companies with up to 100 employees, an IRA account into which both employee and employer can contribute.

Simplified Employee Pensions is retirement plan available to employers and the self-employed. All contributions are tax-deductible.

Single-person 401(k) also called a solo 401(k) and a self-employed 401(k) is a retirement plan that simplifies the administration of a 401(k) enough to make it affordable for single-person companies and very small enterprises.

Sixty-day rollover is a transfer of assets from a 401(k) plan to an individual retirement account during a 60-day period and that assesses a 10 percent early withdrawal penalty unless the rollover is not completed in 60 days.

Social Security formally known as the Federal Old Age, Survivors and Disability Insurance program provides retirement funding and other benefits to participants.

Sole proprietorship is an unincorporated business owned by one person.

Solution providers are companies that provide all-in-one packages for running an online business (usually for a flat monthly fee).

Start-up phase is the period in which a business begins operation, generally the first three months.

Stock is a share of ownership in a company. Stocks come in a variety of types, with different features and objectives.

Stop loss orders is a method of stock buying specifically designed to limit your losses and protect whatever profit you may have earned from a stock.

Summary Plan Description (SPD) is the book of rules that governs your specific 401(k) plan, including when an employee will be eligible to participate and the specifics about how to contribute to the account and how money can be withdrawn.

Surrender value is the amount you receive if you cash out a life insurance policy.

Target date fund is a mutual fund whose allocation of assets is tailored to perform best within a time specific event, like your retirement date.

Tax credit is a reduction in income tax on a dollar-for-dollar basis.

Tax deferred is the income gains generated by investments that do not become taxable until the funds are withdrawn from the account.

Tax-deductible is the quality of income or capital gains generated by investments that can reduce tax liability by the amount deposited into a retirement account.

Taxable income is the earning from an individual's job and investments that are taxable each year.

Teaser cards are credit cards with very low interest rates that last only for a limited amount of time.

Technical analysis is a stock analysis on which a company's trading patterns are charted and analyzed.

Term life insurance is the simplest form of life insurance, as it involves no cash value.

Testamentary trust is a trust, created under a last will and testament that becomes effective only after the grantor dies and the will is admitted to probate.

Timing the market means determining at a particular moment in time, which way the market is going – up or down or sideways.

Treasury securities are issued and backed by the federal government. They come in various forms, including securities, notes, savings bonds, and other formats.

Trustee fees are the cost paid by investors in retirement accounts that can include sales commissions, management, and administration fees.

Trusts are a legal vehicle in which one person (known as the trustee) holds property for another person (known as the beneficiary). This trustee can be a person or a trust company. Trusts are useful in distributing the assets of an estate.

Turnkey business is a business that is ready to go into operation, with all materials, processes, and equipment in place to produce a product or service.

Umbrella insurance is an additional form of liability insurance coverage.

Unearned income is income you don't earn. Common examples are pension and annuity payouts, dividends, and interest and proceeds from life insurance.

URL (Uniform Resource Locator) is another name for a web address.

Value averaging is a variant on dollar-cost averaging that takes into account stock price movement.

Variance is a change or alteration of a zoning rule granted specifically for one person.

Venture capitalists are people or companies that invest in businesses (often technology related)
with the expectation of realizing big profits in the future.

Virtual workers are people who do jobs from their own locations, such as answering your telephone from their home offices rather than from your office.

Waiting period is the time between the onset of a disability and when benefits begin.

Will is a written document that delineates how you want your property distributed after you die.

Withdrawal is a cash value of an asset redeemed from a retirement account.

Work credits are a system to determine Social Security eligibility. You become formally eligible once you have accumulated 40 "work credits."

Yield is the effective rate of interest that a bond pays to investors.

Appendix B

Useful Information

Annual Reports

Investor Guide (*www.investorguide.com/stocklist.cgi)* provides links to thousands of publicly traded companies.

Best Calls *(www.bestcalls.com)* provides access to companies' quarterly earnings press conferences.

Public Register's Annual Report Service *(www.prars.com)* offers both online and hard copy annual reports.

Thomson Investor Net (*www.thomsoninvest.net)* covers more than 7,000 in-depth company reports that are updated twice a month.

Security Exchange Commission (SEC) is the official government site that hosts all financial reports of the publicly traded companies in the United States. The site is at *www.sec.gov /edgar/searchedgar/webusers.htm*

Bonds

Bonds Online (*www.bondsonline.com*) provides charts and historical data that compare the various bond market sectors.

The Bond Market Association *(www.bondmarket.com)* is loaded with information about thousands of bonds and their respective trading history.

Brokers

Charles Schwab *(www.schwab.com)*

Fidelity Investments *(www.jidelity.com)*

T. Rowe Price *(www.troweprice.com)*

Vanguard Group *(www.vanguard.com)*

Budgeting

You can view a sample budget at *www.personalbudgeting.com*. A good resource for developing a budget is available at *www.simpleplanning.net*. The following websites contain good budget tools:

www.flexibleretirementplanner.com
www.smartmoney.com
www.money.com
www.personalbudgeting.com
www.simpleplanning.com
www.tdameritrade.com
www.fidelity.com/myplan

Credit Cards and Credit Scores

To find out about credit card options, visit *www.e-wisdom.com*. The website at *www.cardratings.com* offers a variety of resources to help you understand everything related to credit cards. For a fee, you can find out what your score is at *www.myjico.com*. You can check your credit report at all three bureaus at *www .annualcreditreport.com*. The following websites will provide you with additional information about credit cards and credit scores:

www.cardrating.com
www.cardratings.com
www.myfico.com
www.annualcreditreport.com

Debt Reduction

If you need more advice on reducing your debt, try Barnes & Noble's website *www.barnesandnoble.com)* or Amazon's website *(www.amazon.com)* and browse through their debt-related books. The website at *http://cgi.money.cnn.com/tools/debtplanner/debtplannerjsp* will help you project when you will be debt free. If you are interested in learning more about bankruptcy, go to *www.banhruptcvinfo.com.* Qpicken.com offers a Debt Reduction Planner, an excellent tool for about $50. The following websites will provide you with debt reduction information:

www.defeatthedebt.com
www.cgi.money.cnn.com
www.bankrupcyinfo.com
www.smartmoney.com
www.money.com
www.simpleliving.net
www.debetorsanonymous.org
www.clearbankrupcy.com

Discount Brokers

Accutrade *(www.accutrade.com) 800-494-8939*

American Express (*www.americanexpress.com*) 800-658-4677

Morgan Stanley *(www.morganstanley.com) 212-761-4000*
E*Trade *(www.etrade.com) 800-387-2331*

Fidelity *(wwwjidelity.com) 800-544-8666*

Muriel Siebert *(www.msiebert.com) 800-872-0444*

Schwab *(www.schwab.com) 800-435-4000*

Scottrade *(scottrade.com) 800-619-7283*

Wall Street Access *(www.wsaccess.com) 800-925-5782*

TD Ameritrade *(www.tdameritrade.com) 800-669-3900*

Diversified Investing

Legg Mason's website *(www.leggmason.com)* provides an online questionnaire to help you develop a diversification plan.

Frank Russell Company'{ *www.russell.com)* features a Comfort Quiz to help you allocate your investments.

Fidelity's Asset Diversification Planner *(www.fidelity.com)* offers diversification advice, a risk questionnaire, and model portfolios.

The Intelligent Asset Allocator *(www.eJficientfrontier.com)* offers comprehensive information on how to build a diversified portfolio.

Education

To learn more about federal financial aid for college and how to apply, visit the U.S. Department of Education's website at *www.ed.gov.*

The American Association of Individual Investors offers advice on funds and portfolio management on their website at *www.aaii.com.*

Bloomberg Personal Finance *(www.bloomberg.com)* offers online training when you click on the Bloomberg University module.

Investing Basics *(www.aaii.com/invbas)* offers feature articles about how to start successful investment programs, pick winning stocks, and evaluate your options.

Investor Guide (*www.investorguide.com*) features more than 1,000 answers to frequently asked questions.

Money 101 provides an interactive investment seminar at *www.money.cnn.com*. Money's *www.eldernet.comlmoney.htm* offers tutorials and advice on investing in stocks, mutual funds, and bonds.

Morningstar's University (*www.morningstar.com*) offers a comprehensive investment education program. The Motley Fools offer an investment seminar on their website at *www.fool.com*.

The Mutual Fund Education Alliance is the trade association for no-load funds and offers advice on how to select funds *(www.mfea.com)*.

Vanguard *(www.vanguard.com)* offers online courses that cover the fundamentals of investing in mutual funds.

Estate Planning

If you want to create a basic will on your computer, Quicken offers a software product called WilI Maker that is available in computer stores and at *www.nolo.com*. The following websites will provide you with additional estate planning information:

www.quicken.com
www.nolo.com
www.smartmoney.com
www.money.com
www.kinplinger.com
www.smartmoney.com/retirement
www.mpower.com
www.financialengines.com
www.morningstar.com

Financial Calculators

www.kinplinger.com

www.socialsecurity.gov/estimator
www.fincalc.com
www.dinkytown.com
www.calc.xml
www.dinkytown.com
www.riskgrades.com
www.choosetosave.org/calculators
www.schwab.com
www.troweprice.com/ric

Financial and Economic News

The Bureau of Economic Analysis *(www.bea.gov)* calculates economic indicators such as the gross domestic product and other regional, national, and international data, all of which are displayed on their website.

Census Bureau *(www. census.gov)* provides information about industry statistics and general business conditions.

STAT-USA *(www.stat-usa.gov)* is sponsored by the U.S. Department of Commerce and provides financial information about economic indicators, statistics, and economic news.

Financial Planning Organizations

The American Institute of Certified Public Accountants *(www.aicpa.org)*
Personal Financial Planning Division, 1211 Avenue of the Americas, New York, NY 10036, 800-862-4272

The National Association of Personal Financial Advisors *(www. nap/a. org)* 355 W. Dunbee Rd., Suite 200, Buffalo Grove, IL 60089, 800-333-6659

A website that offers a variety of articles on financial planning is at *ww.money.cnn.com.*

Financial Publications and News Sites

The following websites will provide you with additional financial information and news:

www.money.cnn.com
www.cnnmoney.com
www.simpleplanning.com
www.fidelity.com
www.businessweek.com
www.kinplinger.com
www.morningstar.com
www.kiplinger.com
www.Yodlee.com
www.investools.com
www.quicken.com
www.fidelity.com
www.Smartinvestmentbook.com

Financial Tools

The Financial Center *(wwwfinancia!center.com)* has a section for retirees. Choose United States and then financial planning. Under this category, choose retirement. Schwab *(www.schwab.com)* helps you develop a financial plan with its online calculators, tools, and advice. Virtual Stock Exchange by Market Watch *(www.virtualstock exchange.com)* is a stock-simulation game that allows you to trade shares just as you would in a real brokerage account.

Government Agencies

The following websites will provide you with additional government agency information:

www.irs.gov

www.irs.gov
www.completetax.com
www.medicare.gov
www.socialsecurity.gov/estimator
www.socialsecurity.gov

Home Based Businesses

U.S. Small Business Administration (800) 827-5722; *sba.gov*
American Home Business Association (866) 396-7773
homebusinessworks.com
Entrepreneur.com is an online small business resource center
providing information and advice on products, services and
resources.
Familybusinessmagazine.com offers tips, articles and advice about
starting and operating a family business.
Home-based-business-opportunities.com features hundreds of home
based and small business opportunities listings.
Homebusinessmag.com is an online magazine with information,
advice, tools and links for home business owners.
Powerhomebiz.com provides information, advice and tools for home
business owners.
Sbomag.com is the Small Business Opportunities Magazine
providing readers with the latest small business opportunities news,
information and industry resources.

Index Funds

There are literally hundreds of mutual funds that index every
segment of the market. Here are two of the better funds to consider:
Fidelity Spartan Market Index Fund, which mirrors the Standard &
Poor's 500 (S&P 500) index (800-544-8888) T. Rowe Price Equity
Index Fund, which mirrors the S&P 500 (800-638-5660).

Industry Trends

ABC News *(www.abcnews.com)* features articles on current industry news and market expert commentary. American Society of Association Executives *(www.asaenet.org)* provides high quality industry overviews including briefings of industry trends. Hoovers Online *(www.stockscreener.com)* offer excellent information on industries at their website. *Research* magazine *(www.researchmag.com)* offers helpful references to industry news, columns, and highlights.

Insurance

If you are paying for your own insurance, go to *www.ehealthinsurance.com* to determine if there is a less expensive plan to switch to. The website at *www.nmfn.com* will help you estimate your life span and need for life insurance based on your age, gender, lifestyle, and medical history.

International Investing

The Internet is rich in sources for information on foreign companies. Three websites in particular with useful information are *www.bankofny.com, wwwjpmorgan.com,* and *www.global-investor.com.* Also, FT Market Watch *(wwwftmarketwatch.com)* provides up-to-the minute news on offshore companies and foreign markets.

Investment Advice

The websites at *www.morningstar.com, www.kiplinger.com,* and *www.investools.com* will help you select stocks and mutual funds that meet your investment parameters. Shop around for the best certificate of deposit rates in your area at *www.bankrate.com.* To learn more about home loans, foreclosure prevention, and predatory lending, go to *www.loansafe.org.* Bankrate.com can find the best rates available in your area for motor vehicles.

Bank of America's website *(www.bankamerica.com)* offers a retirement center under the heading Achieve Your Goals on their main menu. It has several useful references for advice for retirees.
Investor Home (*www.investorhome.com*) provides information about the investment process and how to bulletproof your portfolio.

Investment Associations

American Association of Individual Investors *(www.aaii.com)* offers a variety of valuable services to their members, including local chapter meetings in the major metropolitan areas.
The National Association of Investors Corporation (NAIC) is a national association with local chapters throughout the country. Their goal is to help investors develop a disciplined approach to successful investing. For more information, visit their website at *www.better-investing.org*.

Magazines

Business Week(www.businessweek.com) is available online to all of its subscribers.

Forbes (www.forbes. com) is available online and features articles on personal finance and investing.

Fortune (wwwfortune.com) includes special market reports as well as stock and fund quotes.

Kiplinger's (www.kiplinger.com) has a broader scope than many of its competitors. Instead of talking just about investing, *Kiplinger's* moves into other issues of personal business, such as credit card spending, loans, college tuition, and vacation planning. For subscription information, call 800-624-2946.

Newsweek (www.newsweek.com) not only covers the general news but also covers the latest news about the stock market. *SmartMoney* is the" *Wall Street Journal* magazine of personal business" and it's excellent. For subscription information, call 800-444-4204 or visit their website at *www.smartmoney.com.*

Worth columnists, including Peter Lynch, are second to none, and the magazine's regular features are dynamite. For subscription information, call 800-777-1851 or go to
www.worth. com. Money does an excellent job of keeping its readers informed about what's happening in the mutual fund market. For subscription information, visit their website at *www.money.com.*

Motor Vehicle Acquisition

For comprehensive car-buying information, go to *www.edmunds.com, www.autobytelcom,* and *www.carsmart.com.* To get an estimate of used car values, go to the Kelly Blue Book at *www.kbb.com.* Edmunds at *www.cdmunds.com* or eAuto at *www.eauto.com.* If you are interested in purchasing a used vehicle, check out:

Trader Online *(www.traderonline.com)*
 Kelley Blue Book's Classifieds *(www.kbb.com)*
 Online Auto *(www.onlineauto.com)*
Auto Web Interactive *(www.autoweb.com).*

If you are interested in purchasing a new vehicle, check out *www.autosite.com* to find dealer invoice prices or find out about the maintenance records on cars that interest you.

Mutual Fund Companies and Brokers

Charles Schwab *(www.schwab.com)*
Fidelity Investments *(www.jidelity.com)*
T. Rowe Price *(www.troweprice.com)*
Vanguard Group *(www.vanguard.com)*

Mutual Funds

There are almost as many mutual funds to choose from as there are stocks. The following websites will help you find the best ones out there:

CBS Market Watch *(www.marketwatch.com)* provides articles, news, and market data on funds.

MaxFunds (*www.maxfunds.com*) specializes in offering news and statistics on small and little-known funds.

Morningstar (*www.morningstar.com*) is a premier site providing all kinds of information about mutual funds.

Fidelity *(wwwjidelity.com)* offers direct purchase plans for its funds.

Janus *(www.janus. com)* has a family of no-load funds that you can purchase or apply for online.

T. Rowe Price *(www.troweprice.com)* offers direct purchase plans for its funds.

Vanguard *(www.vanguard.com)* has more than eighty funds that you can purchase directly from the company.

News Online

One of the biggest advantages of getting your news online is that you can go to the specific news sector (e.g., Market Watch) without having to thumb through a bunch of paper to get there. Here are several excellent sites to try:

ABC News *(www.abcnews.com)* features business and industry news and market commentary.

Bloomberg Personal Finance *(www.bloomberg.com)* is loaded with timely business news, data, and an analysis of the market.

News Page *(www.newspage.com)* allows you to customize daily news abstracts that it sends to your e-mail address.

Newspapers

Financial newspapers are still a way of life in the stock market's paper-oriented world, although some of them are beginning to make the migration over to the online sector. Here's a rundown of several excellent papers that are out there:

The *Financial Times (wwwft.com)* provides special reports on the market and the different industry sectors.

Investor's Business Daily is a great financial newspaper that publishes important information to help determine the value of a stock. For subscription information, call 800-831-2525 or visit their website at *www.investors.com.*

The *New York Times (www.nytimes.com)* provides a business section that includes quotes and charts, a portfolio management tool, and breaking business news.

USA Today (www.usatoday.com) features a money section that includes investment articles and news, economic information, and information on industry groups.

The *Wall Street Journal* is the Big Kahuna among investment newspapers, although its authority isn't as unquestioned as it used to be. For subscription information, call 800-778-0840 or visit their website at *www.wsj.com.*

Portfolio Management

There are several portfolio management tools that you can use to manage your portfolio. Check out the following websites:

Morningstar (*www.morningstar.com*) provides a portfolio setup menu that is easy to use.

Quicken *(www.quicken.com)* offers a variety of financial tools including an excellent portfolio-management program.

Microsoft (*www.money.msn.com*) offers a wealth of financial data.

Professional Advice

The following websites will provide you with access to professional advisors:

www.napfa.org
www.fpanet.org
www.aicpa.org

Quotes (Stocks and Mutual Funds)

American Stock Exchange (*www.amex.com*) offers quoting services on their website for stocks that are traded on its exchange.

Microsoft Investor (*www.investor.msn.com*) offers a free stock ticker that you can personalize along with portfolio-tracking tools.

The National Association of Securities Dealers *(www. nasdaq.com)* offers quoting services on their website for stocks that are traded on its exchange.

The New York Stock Exchange *(www.nyse.com)* offers quoting services on their website for stocks that are traded on its exchange.

PC Quote *(www.pcquote.com)* offers current stock prices, portfolio tracker, company profiles, and broker recommendations.

Business Week (www.businessweek.com/investor) features applicable information for researching investment opportunities.

Real Estate

Cost-of-living and moving calculators are available at *http://cgi.money.cnn.com/tools*. To calculate mortgage rates and review *Money* magazine articles on real estate, go to *www.usatoday.comlmoney*. The following websites will provide you with additional information on real estate:

www.bankrate.com
www.realestate.msn.com
www.craigslist.com
www.wheretoretire.com

Reducing Expenses

The following websites will provide you with information about how to reduce expenses:

www.carpoolworld.com
www.erideshares.com
www.campusbookretals.com
www.chegg.com
www.billshrink.com
www.energystar.gov

Retirement Planning

Charles Schwab's website will help you develop a retirement plan with their online calculators, tocls, and advice at *www.schwab.com* (click on Advice & Retirement at the top of the menu).
Quicken offers a software product called Will Maker that is available at several computer stores and online at *www.nolo.com.* A retirement budget worksheet is available at *wwwjidelity.com* when you select the Retirement & Guidance option in their main menu.

A retirement calculator can be accessed at *www.usnews.com* when you select the Retirement sub-menu that is under their Money & Business main menu. If you are interested in getting an annuity quote, go to *www.immediateannuities.com.* The following websites will provide you with additional information on retirement planning:

www.flexibleretirementPlanner.com
www.immediateannuities.com
www.quicken.com/retirment/planner
www.kinplinger.com
www.smartmoney.com
www.money.com
www.schwab.com
60 Plus Association at *www.60plus.org*

American Association of Retired People at *www.aarp.org*

Fifty Plus at *www.fifty-plus.net*

Grand Times at *www.grandtimes.com*

Hoover's Online *(www.stockscreener.com)* provides a special module for retirement planning.

Information Seniors at *www.infoseniors.com*

Reverse Mortgages

The following websites will provide you with additional information about reverse mortgages:

www.aarp.com
www.revmort.com/nrmla

Savings Programs

For steps to take to save money, go to *www.themoneykeys.com.* To determine if you are saving enough, go to *www.kiplinger.com*

Shopping and Selling

If you are shopping for an item or selling a household item that would be difficult to get an appraisal on, see what similar items are selling for in the classified advertisements or on *www.ebay.com, www.netmarket.com,* or *www.craigslist.com.* Yellow Page listings are available at *http://search.bigfoot.com* or *www.switchboard.com.* The following websites will provide you with additional information on shopping and buying on the internet:

www.bluefly.com
www.yoox.com

Stock and Mutual Fund Market Timing

The following websites will provide you with additional information on timing the stock and mutual fund markets:

www.schwab.com
www.trowprice.com
vanguard.com
www.fidelity.com
www.fundalarm.com
www.timingthemarket.net
www.stockcharts.com
www.vectorvest.com

Stock Evaluation Programs

Finding out what stock analysts are saying about a stock that you're considering can help you determine if it's the right time to buy. Here are several sites that will get you the information you need:

VectorVest *(www.vectorvest.com)* offers free reports showing what your stocks are really worth, how safe they are, and when to buy, sell, or hold. It's one of the best analyst's sites on the Internet.

S&P Advisor Insight *(www.advisorinsight.com)* allows you to review Standard & Poor's reports for major stocks.

Zacks Investment Research *(www.zacks.com)* reports on what analysts are saying about most of the stocks on the U.S. exchanges.

Stock Exchanges

The American, NASDAQ and New York Stock Exchanges offer a wide variety of investment features that may appeal to you.

American Stock Exchange *(www.amex.com)*.

The National Association of Securities Dealers *(www. nasdaq.com)*.

The New York Stock Exchange *(www.nyse.com)*.

Taxes

For tax deductions, go to *www.bottomlinesecrets.comlextra.* For tax preparation ideas, go to *http://tax.yahoo.comlchecklist.html.*

Travel Websites

www.expedia.com
www.travelocity.com
www.besifares.com
www.budgettravel.com

Web Search Engines

Alta Vista: *www.altavista.com*
Google: *www.google.com*
HotBot: *www.hotbot.com*
Lycos: *uruno.lycos.com*
Yahoo!: *www.yahoo.com*

About the Author & Testimonials

David Rye was the founder of Computech Corporation and later, a director at IBM where he earned an MBA with honors from Seattle University. He is currently president of Western Publications and writes personal finance books from his Goodyear, Arizona office. His award-winning books include *It's Not Too Late To Rescue Your 401(k)*, *Stop Managing and Lead*, *Starting Up*, and *1001 Way to Inspire Yourself*. He also consultants baby boomers to show them how to get the most out of their retirement plans.

"Perfect for boomers who are about to retire and are thinking about retiring ... in a standard of living they can be comfortable with."
Dr. T.K. Nelsen, Stanford University

"A great book in a writing style that is highly interactive where each chapter challenges to reader to expand their role in getting out of debt ... you'll learn how you can retire in $tyle."
Dale Moser, President and CEO, Niwot Technology, Inc.

"A hands-on book that dramatically illustrates how anyone can enjoy a financially free life after they retire."
Mark Kruger, Ph.D., Creative Thinking Seminars

"... adds an element of real world reality to the retirement process that is truly unique and refreshing."
A.J. Osorio, President, Llanos Publishing